I AM
GOD'S CHILD,

(The ABR Formula!)

Ask, Believe, Receive!

BASED ON A TRUE STORY!

DAPHINE L. KENNEDY

This written work is based on a true story.

First Paperback Edition 2020

ISBN: 978-0-578-68732-2

Library of Congress Control Number: 2020910711

Published by Daphine L. Kennedy, St. Louis MO

Email: daphine.kennedy@gmail.com

Credits:

Charles Wartts, Editor

Graphic Design by Elaine A. Young, hopdezin@swbell.net

TABLE OF CONTENTS

DEDICATION IV
ACKNOWLEDGMENTS VI
PROLOGUE VII

DEDICATION

This body of work is dedicated to anyone who has been faced with any form

of adversity; but most importantly this body of work is dedicated to all of

my siblings as well as to any child that has experienced being an orphan who

was placed in the fostercare system, residential facility (children's home), or

judicial system. I dedicate this book to those of you who come from or who

are now in poverty stricken environments that are plagued with drugs and

violence. This book is also dedicated to those of you who have lost a loved

ones, or who may have a family member who has struggled or is struggling

with addiction. Moreover, this book is dedicated to those of you who have

chosen to go after your dreams without fear. Let's express ourselves by

taking action so that we may create the change that we want to see by making

our voices heard, not just in our families and communities, but throughout

the world. This book is intended to not only inspire but to bring love

and unity. In order to have unity we must know and understand that there is

no place for racism, nor systemic racism. Yes, I am Black!

I am also a spirit being having a human experience just like you.

I am God's child, I am!...I am You!

ACKNOWLEDGMENTS

I would like to thank God (I Am) for conspiring with me to bring this book into reality. I want to thank my mother, Blanche Denise Kennedy, without you none of this would be possible. Though it has been years, I can hear your voice clearly now Mama, saying, "I too am God's Child." Thank you to my children D'Chyra and Brandon. I love you. It was your love that gave me strength day after day. It was seeing your faces that pushed me toward my dreams so that we may see a better tomorrow. I would also like to acknowledge all of my siblings: Dwayne aka Bam; Esqerra aka Shaunta; Marcus and Keanca. Special thanks to my big sister, Demetrica aka Buttercup for inspiring me to read and for the precious gift of sharing your writings with me. Thank you Buttercup and Shaunta for listening to all my silly jokes during the pain; it was the laughter that eased the pain. Thank you to Ms. A aka Angela Bryant for being that mother figure, for teaching me to never give up and to always believe in myself.

A very special thank you to the late great Ms. Maya Angelou and another great woman, Ms. Alice Windom, for meeting me on my journey and for connecting me with a friend so that I would able to publish this work. I know now that these blessed connections were all about divine alignment! Thank you to the friend who introduced me to books that helped to change my mindset. Much gratitude to the man and woman whom I encountered in the bookstore for their advice and words of encouragements. Thank you to DeVon Franklin for being my "virtual mentor." Your motivation kept me going as you wisely encouraged me to become the author of my own life movie. Thank you to my editor, Mr. Charles Wartts, for the many conversations during which you shared your thoughts and experiences—and thank you so much for believing in me. I would also like to thank Ms. Elaine Young for her graphic design work and for bringing my vision to life. Thank you to all the individuals I've encountered on my journey; it was these experiences that shaped and molded me. I am a spirit being having a human experience. I am God's child, I Am!

PROLOGUE

MANY OF US ask the question, "Who am I?" or "What is my purpose or calling here on this earth?" We become wanderers in search of fulfillment, happiness, and abundance. While searching for our soul's purpose we must stop wandering and wondering and get clear about who we really are. We are God's children. God wants you to increase your faith in Him so that you may live your best life, the life that He has planned for you. You are from the Creator. Therefore, you also have the ability to create!

So what are you waiting for? You have the power to create the life that you desire. May I introduce to you the ABR Formula? Ask, Believe, and Receive! Sounds too simple, huh? Well, first you must have faith in order for this formula to work while you're on your life's journey. What is faith? Faith is the substance of things hoped for, the evidence of things not seen; it is a strong conviction about the shape of things that have not yet happened in your life. One must have unwavering faith because the Bible tells us that "faith without works is dead." In addition, you must learn to be of service to others. It is through your service to others that you'll find fulfillment. Don't be afraid to give of yourself. Will there be challenges or obstacles on your journey to finding your true life's purpose? Absolutely! No soul escapes life's experiences, which at times we face without warning.

Often there is no time for preparation because life unfolds the way it chooses without our permission. Life will unfold for you just as God has planned it. Not to punish or hurt you, however. Rather, it is because God loves you and knows what's best for you. Without a doubt, you will be met by adversity at some time or another on your journey. Regardless of how hard, tragic, stressful, or disturbing the situation or circumstances you may be called upon to endure, get still and know that these obstacles are only meant to shape and mold you for who God has called you to be or for what God has called you to do. Will there be constant change? Yes, absolutely, because change is inevitable. When life happens, one must learn to pray. Then, have faith and believe that your prayers have been heard by your Creator.

Moreover, know that there is power in prayer. This infinite power listens to you and will also aid you upon your request. Therefore, be mindful of what you ask for (as well as the story you tell yourself) because the Divine Spirit listens. God will deliver to you whatever you ask of Him—but only in His own perfect timing and according to your faith. You will get only "what you believe you will receive, believing that you have already received" (Mark 11:24.). Therefore, monitor your thoughts for they will manifest in your life whether conscious or unconscious. For "as a man thinketh in his heart, so is he" (Proverbs 23:7).

A very important question we must ask is what story we are telling ourselves about our life's experiences. Stop telling yourself the story with shame and guilt attached to it as I did prior to God showing me the true story of my life and how He'd kept me. Negative thoughts about who I was left me drained and stagnant, lacking self-belief and a sense of self-worth. I was even convinced that I couldn't accomplish the task of writing this book. My negative thinking left me doubting whether I was capable or deserving of the life I'd envisioned for myself and my family. When such thoughts would come up, I'd often rely on the power of "I Am" (God). I would immediately cancel out my negative thinking by repeating to myself: "I am worthy! I am deserving! I am God's child!"

VIII

Prior to God's revelation of my true story, the story I told myself was that I was an orphan, which caused me to feel embarrassed and ashamed of the many calamities that my siblings and I had endured. However, what I know now is that I am God's child, and that I was forced to confront several heartbreaking experiences in order to prepare me for something greater. What happened was that God immediately showed me my life in reverse. Yes, in reverse! You see we live life going forward but we only understand it when we look back—after we've already faced many tests and trials.

Always remember that nothing just happens. You see, first I had to go through the storm, traveling to and through many unfamiliar places and personal experiences. I was abandoned by my father; witnessed my mother being addicted to drugs; lived in deplorable conditions; was separated from my siblings; lost loved ones; and escaped domestic violence. I also had to rise up to defeat depression and anger, which allowed me to open myself up to the healing power of self-love. Finally, I had to break free from my own poverty mindset of lack and scarcity.

Yes, there were some horrible things that I had to endure in order to give true testimony about the hurdles I've had to overcome. However, I know now that all of these were placed in my path so that I could fulfill my life's purpose and manifest the book which had already been ordained and planned for me by my Divine Father (God), the Creator.

Now I want to share with you how I manifested my book, which placed me on the path to my destiny. Wherever you are, look around you. You will see things which were created by someone else's thoughts. Our thoughts are a gift to us from our Creator, God. Now, let's get back to how God conspired with me to help me to manifest my book, which is about the Kennedys. No, not the rich and famous Kennedy family whom you all know or have heard about. But my family—the Kennedys—who were also born rich. Rich in laughter, that is. However, both families were called upon to face many adversities.

There are millions of families just like mine who come from or who are now in poverty stricken environments that are plagued by drugs and violence. Many of our family members have fallen victim to addictions—be it alcohol, drugs, or even gun violence, which often destroy both families and communities. This destructive plague then leaves our children to fend for themselves or they turn to the streets, making it inevitable that they will end up in the foster care system or the criminal justice system in most cases.

Be that as it may, always remember that poverty, drug addiction, nor any of life's calamities can define who you are. Who you really are. You too are God's child. Prior to writing this book I was not clear about the power I possessed within. My lack of understanding about the inner power I possessed caused me to make many unconscious negative decisions that I had to learn from. One will continue to be met with the same life lesson until that lesson is received or learned.

Therefore, you must pay attention and receive the lessons or messages that are necessary for your growth. Which is why it is imperative that we learn to make better choices. Lessons learned through our decision-making process shapes our character, molds our purpose, and prepares us for the life we are destined to live. Life lessons come in order to help us find our purpose or calling. I was once one of those wandering souls who had no idea about what my purpose or calling was. For years I searched without direction as I moved from one place to another. Now as I look back over my life, I can see clearly that the presence of God was always there with me. I Am God's child, a spirit being having a human experience!

Though I was not consciously aware of who I was as a child, as

I grew into adolescence and adulthood my soul yearned for purpose. I believe that every life was created for a specific purpose. I believe I was called to write this book, which has led me to my purpose. My purpose here on this earth is to serve. And so is yours. Ask yourself: "How can I serve or make an impact on someone else's life?" Before being enlightened I would wake up in the morning dreading going to work or repeating the same routine day after day. Not having a college degree, I'd managed to land a job at the United States Postal Service. And still I was unhappy and surrounded by debt. I wanted to have joy in my life. I knew I was there for a reason and that all my steps were being ordered by God, so I continued to thank Him daily for allowing me a way to provide for my family.

At the same time, I was desperately seeking a better way to not only provide for my family, but I also wanted to be a blessing to others. I wanted joy, fulfillment, and abundance. I wanted to inspire other individuals to think themselves out of unhappy situations and out of poverty stricken environments. Throughout my life I'd heard people complaining about being in debt, about being frustrated and overwhelmed by life's challenges. Take action now! Know that you are sent here on this earth for a purpose. Have faith in our Creator. He has blessed you with supernatural abilities. You must learn to trust God despite the challenges that confront you. God has not only given you life, our Creator has blessed each and every one of us with certain abilities and talents. It is a gift to us from our Father. Your gifts will make a way for you. Our Creator is waiting to pour His blessings out upon you. So serve, give, and help someone else!

Many of us want a better life. Therefore one must be willing to take action, stay on task, and complete the call of action placed on your life. To quote the late, great Dr. Wayne Dyer, "Change your thoughts, change your life." In order to live your best life you must change the way you think. Yes, that's right! In order to change your life, you must change your way of thinking. I began changing my life by first changing my thoughts, by using "I Am!" affirmations. Now that I am writing and sharing my story with the world, I wake up every morning feeling fulfilled. This is because I am now living my purpose.

I am writing this book with the faith that I will be able to inspire, enlighten, or help someone overcome their life challenges. Though my life's path has often been turbulent, no matter where I end up I'd always tell myself: "There's something more in life for you." You see, I possessed this strong feeling of knowing and believing that there was something more for me to accomplish. Feeling is believing, and if you believe you should expect. Expect that everything you desire is on its way. And if you choose to live in purpose and obey the call of action for your life, then God will allow you to live the life that you deserve, according to His will. There is power in using "I Am!" affirmations. It is these two words that strengthened me to never give up, which propelled me to continue my quest for a more fulfilling life.

Therefore, monitor your thoughts as well as what you speak, for these two words can create your reality and give to you whatever you attach to them. "For death and life are in the power of the tongue" (Proverbs 18:21.). Moreover, for those of you who are not sure about what your purpose or calling is, get still and ask yourself how can you be of service to others using your God given talents or gifts. In addition, there are times when you may be called to do a thing, such as being a voice for the voiceless or shedding light upon injustice. You may even be called to bring awareness to a particular issue or cause which you may possess no knowledge of at the time. And according to the great Ms. Oprah Winfrey, if you are called to do a thing and don't have the knowhow, you should simply be obedient to the call. Also, rest assured that God (the Creator) will bring forth the manifestation of that thought or idea according to your faith and intention. Therefore, be of good cheer, believing that God ("I Am") is always guiding you along the way, conspiring to help you fulfill that purpose or calling.

Now, will life's journey always be comfortable? Absolutely not, because life is meant to shape and mold you. Life has its way of bringing forth situations in order to transform some characteristics in us that we lack. This means our prejudices, racism, judging, unkind ways, lack of empathy, jealousy, impatience, and selfishness, etc. This transformation could also mean learning to love others. Life will often shape you in a manner that will increase your faith, build strength, and help you endure in order to bear witness so that you may be used by God to give true testimony. God may even allow you to witness miracles so that you might believe.

Furthermore, the turbulence I would grow up to experience in adulthood was extremely painful, but I've managed to make it through with God on my side. I've had divine guidance, help—and most importantly—unconditional love from God during my journey here on this earth as I look back over my life. It is also my intention to bring awareness, enlightenment, and inspiration to anyone who thinks that God has forgotten about them. In sharing my story, I hope that you will see how God has conspired to not only help me write this book, but to also overcome many adversities. The Divine Spirit is always present, and most importantly, this Divine Power lives within you. You may refer to this infinite power as God, I Am, Jehovah, Allah, Yahweh, The Universe, The Source, The Most High, The Creator, The Almighty, The Divine Spirit, etc.

While I respect all faiths, it is my belief that there is only one

God who has created all things. The God who has given us His son Jesus Christ who died for our sins, and who is my personal Lord and Savior. However, due to the many religions, traditions, and cultures of this world, you may choose to call this infinite power by one of many names. This book is not intended to cause conflict about religion nor between religions. My intention is to bring unity in the hope that we all may agree and believe that there is surely a power that's greater than ourselves who loves us all. Therefore, it is my opinion that one cannot choose just one name to describe or to refer to our Creator, for His works and powers far exceed the human mind. In Exodus 3:14, God says unto Moses: "I AM THAT I AM." May I submit for your consideration that God (I Am) is also working on your behalf even as you're reading these words right now! Yes, you too can experience the power of divine alignment!

The story of my life seemed to be a rather turbulent experience as I searched for my purpose. Then one day, after being inspired, my spirit or inner voice spoke to me: "Serve. Share your testimony. Don't be ashamed. Write the book. Don't be afraid. Dream big. Live your best life. It is your birthright, for you are my child!" Prior to my enlightenment, I had many fearful reservations about sharing my story. Plus, I'd never written a book, nor did I have any prior experience in writing. Still I felt compelled to act. I instantly knew that I was to share my testimony. Not only was I to share this testimony, but I was to put this testimony in book form and send it out into the universe. In doing so, I was placed on the path to achieve the destiny that awaited me.

As I changed my thoughts, my life began to change. As I told my truth and shared my testimony without shame, my heart began to soften. When the shame went away, I no longer felt embarrassed. I began feeding my mind with positive thoughts and "I Am!" affirmations. Monitoring my negative thinking was not an easy task. I would immediately become aware of my negative thoughts and replace them with positive ones. Battling negative thinking was a struggle for me because it came from years of negative programming. I had to learn how to be more positive when processing my thoughts. I was determined to let the "old self" die in order to birth my authentic self. It was now up to me to free my mind, as it was often worried and racing with thoughts. Being fearful and worried rendered me powerless. The process of letting go of fear and negative thinking, was challenging, but I did not give up.

Though I was willing to do the work, I could not accomplish such a task as battling the mind without God's help. It was my Father who created me. Therefore, it is my Father who has the ability to restore my mind as well as my faith. And you too must be willing to do the work while asking for God's help. My "new mind" brought forth a sense of peace that I couldn't understand. I began feeding my faith with God's word, which transformed me, the "old self." I was filled with joy, immediately knowing that it was not me, but "I Am" (God) replacing the old mind with a new mind.

"Who am I now?" I thought. "Same body, new mind," I whispered to myself in awe. Surely I am made new, I sensed. "A new me?" I asked, questioning the new mind or spirit within my body. My new mind instantly connected with this new feeling of peace. And in that moment of consciousness there was a feeling of knowing that I'd discovered my true self. "I am a spirit being having a human experience," I said consciously. Thereafter, I began my quest in search of my purpose and calling. I even began to wonder about the birth name that had been given to me. Who was I without this name? It was my mother who gave birth to me. But it was the Spirit of God that made me, and "the breath of the Almighty that gives me life" (Job 33:4.).

In that moment I began to weep. "Who am I?" I cried. "Speak to me Father…who am I? What is my purpose here?" My tears fell as I waited for answers.

Then a subtle voice replied: **Why do you weep?**

Daughter, you are my child and I love you. I am your Father and the Creator of all things. I send you upon the earth in hopes that you yourself will find your purpose. "I Am" has placed gifts and talents within all of His children. Believe that these gifts and talents will manifest once you have made a conscious decision to serve with good intentions. First, I must shape and mold you so that my light may shine through you. You will forget that you are spirit in body form. "I Am" will remind you that you too are a powerful being. Therefore, you must learn to operate from that being which is spirit. For you are my child, created perfect in my image. Though life will not be perfect for you because you too will sin, and therefore fall short of my glory.

Throughout your life you will feel alone and unsure of your purpose. My child, there will be tragedies, trials, setbacks, hardships, loss, and disappointments. You will experience all of these. Have faith. Trust me, Daughter. "I Am" is within you, thus "I Am" is everywhere you are: guiding, leading, and directing you towards your destiny. Know that "I Am" works everything out for the good of those who believe in Me. Everything that has happened and that will happen has already been ordained by Me, your Father. For it is My Will for your life as I have planned it. Lean not on your own understanding. For everything that has happened to you has been for your greater good. Remember there are no coincidences. Nothing just happens. Everything is orchestrated by Me, your Father. "I Am" will bestow mercy, favor, and grace upon you during your journey

in finding your purpose. Daughter, I give you free will, so choose and be of good merit. Know that "I Am" is within you; therefore, I will always be with you. I will never leave you nor forsake you. I Am the Creator of all who knows all things. Therefore, know I Am That I Am. Daughter, you too are able to create. And without the infinite power that I've stowed within you, know that you of yourself can do nothing. It is "I Am" (God) who does these great works through you. Find, serve, and fulfill your life's purpose. Believe my child that nothing is impossible. "I Am" has made all things possible for those that believe in Me.

And Daughter, He said to me as I sat quietly in solitude.

"Yes, Father," I said cautiously.

Love, my child, as "I Am" has loved you. Forgive wholeheartedly as "I Am" has forgiven you. Fear not nor worry. Enjoy life's blessings which may seem to be in disguise in your darkest hour; for your faith will be tested in this life. Daughter, He said softly, checking for my attentiveness.

"Yes, Father," I said, hanging onto His every word.

Be still and know that I am God. Therefore, accept the mother and the life that I have chosen for you. Now go and know that I am...

1

In The Storm

I WAS BORN in 1981 in Memphis, Tennessee. Life as I knew it was going well. At age 5, I remember being a happy child, full of laughter. My mother was 19, a mother of three, and unwed. She was no longer with my father. And still everything seemed to be okay. At least it seemed that way as I call back the memory of the story that I am now sharing with you.

We stayed in an apartment complex. I remember the day my big brother, sister, and I came in and noticed a big safe in the middle of the living room. We were in awe, having never seen anything like it before. We were amazed by all the money and silver coins all over the place. Clueless yet curious, we picked up and played with the coins. I don't remember hearing Mama or anyone saying stop, don't touch. Moments later we heard shattering glass along with a loud bang! It was the sound of the door and windows being kicked in. In fear, we cried and screamed. The apartment was being raided. Some guys were being led out in handcuffs, and police were everywhere. I was not yet old enough to understand the reason for the raid. And I still don't remember seeing Mama. Where was she? We were afraid. I don't remember what happened next. My mother was present and yet not present. Life as we knew it would change forever.

Shortly afterwards, we left Memphis to move to St. Louis, Missouri where my grandmother lived. She was married to a railroad worker, my grandfather. On this cold day the snow was falling rapidly. My big brother Bam and my big sister Buttercup and I were completely unaware of the tragedy that had just happened to us or the whirlwind of troubles we would now have to face.

We found ourselves on a two-lane highway in the midst of a snow storm. Yet somehow we were still anticipating this new move. A strange man was driving us to St. Louis. Mama was in the car with us as well. We were sitting quietly in the backseat when suddenly the car slid underneath an 18-wheeler truck. Terrified and gripped by fear, we began screaming and crying. The front end of the car was stuck under the huge truck. No one was hurt or injured, thank God. However, this snow storm would always remind us of the move to Grandma's house.

We would always remember this ride to St. Louis. But for whatever reason, the man who was driving us there was no longer with us.

The snow fell upon our eyelids as the brisk wind blew across our little faces. Now we were out in the cold, walking a long stretch of highway as cars drove by. We were quietly listening to the sound of tires that rolled along the wet pavement at steady speeds. I lifted my head up and noticed Mama's face. I couldn't make out any emotions. She seemed completely detached as she held her thumb up, hoping to hitchhike us a ride the remainder of the way.

Finally, we got a ride from a trucker who also drove an 18-wheeler. We rode some distance before he eventually dropped us off at a rest stop. We were cold, tired, exhausted, and hungry when a stranger offered to pay for a hotel and food. I can only imagine what Mama felt. Or did she feel? We loved Blanche, our dear mother. And as long as we were

2

with her we figured everything would be okay. Finally, we made it to St. Louis. Life for us would now be "normal," or so we thought.

The adventure of getting to my Grandma Rose's place was rather turbulent, yet interesting. We were heading straight to the inner city. My grandmother lived on the north side of St. Louis. In the ghetto, as some would call it. I remember spending our days there playing hopscotch, double Dutch, "red light, green light" and other childhood games to entertain one another. I also remember running in front of the television or unplugging the Nintendo while my brother was playing Duck Hunt. We would be laughing and running to avoid my big brother's wrath if he caught us.

During the 1980's, the selling and use of crack cocaine was taking over black communities. Crack cocaine became the biggest epidemic of that era. My little mind could not comprehend the world around me. Nor could I understand the dynamics of the relationship between the two main women in my life. My mom and grandmother's relationship seemed strained. But at that young age I was not really sure why. What I did know was that a good meal always awaited us from Grandma. I also knew how much my siblings and I enjoyed laughter and just being silly. My grandma would say, "Stop that giggling at the table."

Grandma was nice and stern, too. We knew Grandma didn't play. She had a very nice place. It was clean, well-furnished, and grandma always had plenty of food. She lived in a four-family flat. No front yard. There were two bedrooms, which meant my sister, brother, and I would share one bed. We adjusted to the move and started school.

Soon after, my siblings and I would find out that crack cocaine had also reached our family. Even the schools began to raise children's awareness about drugs and started a "Just Say No To Drugs" program.

A few of the children seemed to know more about Mama than we did. On the walk home from school one day, the kids began to chant, "Yo mama on crack rock!" We weren't sure what they meant, and continued our walk home. My big brother Bam who knew more than we did, said to us, "Keep walking." Then another kid yelled, "We saw yo mama coming out the crack house." We continued walking. When we finally made it home I asked Buttercup: "Is Mama on crack?"

"I don't know," she said. "Be quiet before we miss the show." We sat down with our eyes glued to the television, watching our favorite TV show, "Punky Brewster," oblivious to the fact that we would soon be without our mom, just like Punky. Time went on, and soon Mama was pregnant again. She didn't seem happy. We didn't know where she would go. She would leave for days at a time. We would miss her, and Grandma would say, "She'll be back." We loved Mama and longed for her. I don't remember many conversations with her. Only her smile and laughter. We were left for Grandma Rose to raise. I never heard Grandma complain. My grandpa was a rather quiet man. He loved us, too. He was a provider, making sure we were never hungry. There were now four of us. Grandma was a strong woman to be raising all of us. Seem like Mama was just dropping off babies.

Soon there were five of us. My grandmother and grandfather somehow made ends meet along with the help of the food stamps Mama received from welfare. In addition, Grandma Rose made sure we went to church every Sunday, looking rather polished I must say. She would "press" our hair. And she loved to use Vaseline petroleum jelly on our faces, as well as polish our shoes with it. Grandma would send us to church while she stayed home to cook Sunday dinner. The church

4

members would make sure we behaved, being that we loved to laugh.

Buttercup and I would find humor in almost everything. But Grandma would make sure we had an awareness of The Most High God. Well, by that time we knew our mama was a crackhead. Just as the society around us had deemed her. She would stay gone for weeks at a time now. We were so excited whenever she would come back that we didn't ask her any questions. She was pregnant again, and would soon be leaving my baby sister in the arms of my grandmother. Grandma was now raising six children, two boys and four girls. One day I would walk into the house to find Grandma smoking a cigarette. Grandma didn't smoke. I guess the stress of it all was becoming too much for her to bear. Grandma would hide her cigarettes in the kitchen cabinet and smoke while Grandpa was away at work. We never knew if she was sick prior to smoking, because she never complained.

She continued to care for us as usual. Later, Grandma Rose would be diagnosed with lung cancer. Losing her battle to cancer, she died in the late 1980's. Before she died, my siblings and I went to see her. There, at her bedside, she told us that she loved us. She left us with our grandfather, the only other person who could keep us. So living with Grandpa became our reality. Mama was strung out, a dope fiend. We were all clear about that now. My grandfather was our sole provider. Taking care of six small children alone must have been overwhelming for him. So the next time Mama showed up, he left us with her.

Still, he would come to check on us and bring us food whenever he could. I believe our dire circumstances took its toll on Grandpa Eddie. The last time I saw my grandfather he had become very frail. Soon, he died also. We had to grow up fast. Especially since Buttercup, my big sister, was now left to play the mother role. We were just a year apart. Some days we would make it to school. But we missed a lot of school. Most of the time we went to school unkempt. Mama would be gone for weeks at a time, leaving us with no food.

My siblings and I would get into spats with each other over who would go ask for free donuts. "I went the last time. Now it's your turn to go ask," Buttercup said.

"I always go," said Bam.

So I walked down to the local donut shop in hopes that they would give us free donuts again. But the workers at the shop cheerfully gave us donuts without asking questions. They already knew about Mama's addiction.

Childhood seemed to pass right by me. My thoughts were no longer childlike. It was like being pushed into survival mode. My siblings and I had to take care of each other. Being without gas or electric power, food, diapers, clean clothes, etc., was taking a toll on us. To make matters worse, we had plumbing problems because the toilet would no longer flush, which caused maggots to form. We would stuff sheets underneath the bathroom door to cover the odor. The smell and the sight of our stagnant waste would make anybody nauseous. Our situation was deplorable and mind-boggling, to say the least. Nobody came to check on us.

"Where is she? Where is she??" I'd burst out in a fit of anger as Buttercup cried and Bam rode his bike in the dark in search of her. We needed her. My baby sister and brother needed milk and diapers. We waited and waited, looking for her as every car passed and thinking she might be every figure we saw from a distance. Sometimes we would yell for her from the upstairs window that we kept open to rid the house of the odor of human waste.

"Mama! Mama! Mamaaaaa!!! We would call out for her in the night while also yelling "Bingo!" as a nice car drove by that we liked. As we waited, desperately hoping Mama would appear, our shouts ricocheted back to us only as an echo. Plus, our hopes began to dim as our little voices bounced off the brick buildings that surrounded us. At times Bam would leave to go ask whomever he knew for food or money. Meanwhile Buttercup and I looked after our younger siblings. As the middle child, I was silent, stuck in the midst of it all. I knew we needed help, but I could only imagine the pressure my big brother and sister felt. We were as close as any siblings could be, so we recognized the suffering each of us was feeling as we cried tears of sorrow.

In spite of our sorrow, we soothed ourselves with laughter and entertainment by telling jokes, playing "red light, green light," or hide-go-seek in the dark. It became our daily task to find food or something to drink. We ate sugar sandwiches, mayo sandwiches, and syrup sandwiches as we scoured the cabinets for whatever we could eat. We would also cut up bedsheets to use as diapers for the little ones and put sugar and water in their bottles to substitute for milk. We did whatever we had to in order to get through the day. The night hours seemed hardest because there was no electricity. When we could no longer bear Mama's absence, my big brother, sister, and I decided it was in our best interests to call the police. When he arrived, however, he didn't come inside the apartment. We told him we were hungry, and that our mom had not come home in days. He bought us pizza, diapers, and milk. He also told us to "give her another day" because if he took us, we would all be split up, and he didn't want that to happen.

We were happy that the policeman came, but more excited about the fact that we had food for the night. Well, Mama did show up the following day. But we didn't question her. Back then we were taught never to question grown-ups, or else!

As a 7-year-old girl, and the middle child, I had no idea what I was supposed to think or feel. Being seen and not heard as a child was just the way it was back then. Not long after, we learned that our mother's addiction was demanding that she sell her body for drugs, which included abandoning us time after time. By the time I was 8 years old, I was told what it meant "to turn a trick." My little eyes saw things no child should see. During this period my siblings and I experienced what it was like to live at different homeless shelters. We received help from The Salvation Army, Rev. Larry Rice's shelter, women's shelters, and shelters run by churches, to name a few. "Thank you Father for allowing us to take refuge in those safe havens You placed there for us!

However, those places, nor us, ever stopped Mama from wanting her drugs. In fact, nothing could stop her from using—not even our love for her or her love for us! We didn't care about yearly celebrations like birthdays or holidays. We knew we wouldn't be receiving anything unless a church helped Mama out. Whatever we received, it was for all six of us to share. Our Christmas and Thanksgiving dinners were spent standing in long lines at a church along with the homeless and other families without food. I remember being very happy that we were being served so much food. When you don't know when or where your next meal will be coming from, you eat as much as you can.

Crack cocaine was bigger than Mama. This drug controlled her life, and we were along for the ride. Thing is, I still don't remember her saying much. Mama would leave without explanation. "I'll be back," was all she would say. And yet our love for her never wavered. Did she know she was hurting us? Not in terms of direct physical abuse, but mentally and emotionally. We knew that we would be fending for ourselves during her absence. We played and entertained each other during the day and watched television at night by using our neighbor's electricity with a really long extension cord. Our house was completely without power.

When the TV shows Mash and Star Trek went off, we would fall asleep. When we got tired from waiting up for Mama, we knew she wasn't coming back that particular night. We continued to miss a lot of school. And when we did attend, we would get into fights trying to defend our mom or because of our shabby clothes and appearance. Mama could only afford to buy "Buddies" (very cheap shoes), that the kids would tease us about. We would sometimes walk the long way home just to avoid the taunts, but to no avail. My big brother Bam would always say, "Keep walking unless they put their hands on you." That was our cue, which meant if one fights, we all fight. We all knew that rule. And if we didn't help one another, we would have to deal with Mama. We stuck together no matter what.

But the day came when we got tired of waiting for Mama. My older siblings and I decided to call the police again. We asked each other repeatedly, "Are you sure? Are you sure you wanna do this?" We all decided that it was what we should do. We were without food, gas, electricity, clean clothes, and the living conditions were gross. Still, we didn't know what to expect. We all shed tears. What would happen to us now?

When the police arrived, so did the fire department as well as the local news vans equipped with cameras and microphones. Time seemed to stand still. Everyone will know now! Everyone will know about Mama now, I thought. I remember crying for my sisters and brothers. "Don't take them away!" I cried, screamed, and pleaded. Although those demands came out of my mouth with such force, they only fell on deaf ears. There was no turning back. I was the child that didn't say much but felt the most. We were now in the custody of the Department of Family Services (DFS).

We arrived at a local youth center where we were bathed and fed. It was decided that we would be split up. My baby brother and sister— Marcus and Keanca—an infant and a toddler, would stay together. My other two sisters and I stayed together. And my big brother, who was about 11, was later released to his biological father. There were no fathers who came to claim the rest of us. Where was Mama? I wondered. What will she do now that we are in this place? A nice lady tried to reassure my sisters and me that we were safe now, and that we would be okay.

However, the three of us would later be taken to our first foster home. We had to stay with an older lady who was quite mean. She wouldn't allow us to play. But even worse, she gave us cereal with ants in it for breakfast. When she walked out of the kitchen, I raced to the pantry where the cereal was kept and ants were everywhere. When we told her there were ants in the cereal, she did nothing about it. Neither of us ate the ant cereal. Instead, we managed to find humor in that situation as well. "Ant cereal?" we laughed and giggled as the ants swam through the milk. After about a week with her, the social worker arrived to check on us. We told her about the "ant cereal" ordeal and how unhappy we were. She removed us immediately.

10

"Have you heard from our Mama? Is she coming to get us?" we asked the social worker.

"Yes, I have," she told us. "Your mother has some things to do before you can go back with her. She has to go to rehab, have suitable housing, etc.," she said. She also let us know that she wasn't able to find a home that was able to accept all three of us, and that we would have to be separated. My eyes swelled with tears. I glanced at my sisters, watching the heavy flow of tears run down their faces in a steady stream as the thought of being separated began to sink in. Still crying, I whispered to my big sister Buttercup.

"You scared?"

"No," she replied. "Are you scared?"

"No," I replied as we both cried harder, letting each other know that we were both scared.

2

Be A Big Girl

DURING THE RIDE to my second foster home, I decided to sit up straight. I know where I am, I thought to myself. I began to dry my tears, knowing I was close to Grandma's house. I said my goodbyes to both my sisters. I was no longer able to hold back the tears as we parted. Soon I would be greeted by my new foster mother, Ms. Garrett. She was really kind, and the apartment was very welcoming. To my knowledge, she didn't have any children. It was just she and I. She kept the apartment very tidy and was also a great cook, reminding me of Grandma.

I thought about my sisters and brothers daily. I missed them terribly, and I longed for Mama every day. I started school, and I was a bus rider. While sitting on the school bus, I began to memorize the route. My plan was to go find Mama. I missed her real bad and wanted her to somehow get us back. Finally, the day came when I would act on my plan. This particular day I did not get on the bus to go back to Ms. Garrett's house. Instead, I mixed in with all of the children who walked home. I headed for the route that I'd memorized. Soon I recognized the streets near Grandma's house, and took off running with everything that was in me.

I made it! I told myself, my heart still pounding. But then I saw that Grandma's house had been boarded up. So I banged on the downstairs neighbor's door.

"Mr. Jones, have you seen my Mama?" I asked as he opened the door. "Do you know where I can find her?" I was out of breath.

He stood still, looking at me in a state of shock. "Yes! Check Aunt Carrie May's house," he said.

Aunt Carrie May was my mother's friend who was known by everyone in the neighborhood because of her drunkenness. Everyone loved her, including me. She too would give us food at times, when Mama wasn't around. I raced down to her house. The door was already open. I pulled the screen door. "Mama!!!" I screamed, my heart pounding faster, my eyes filled with tears. And there she stood right in front of me. Tears rolled down my cheeks. I leaped onto her, wrapping my arms and legs around her tightly. I cried inconsolably, not wanting to ever let her go. She kissed me, wiping my tears away in an effort to calm me down.

"How did you get here?" she asked.

"I ran Mama…and I don't ever wanna go back!"

She hesitated. "I have to take you back, baby. I will get in a lot of trouble if I don't. I want you to be a big girl for me until I come back for y'all," she said.

All I could do was cry. I felt powerless. We got a cab back to Ms. Garrett's place. At the door, Mama reassured me that she would come back. She kneeled down to hug and kiss me goodbye. Ms. Garrett was not upset with me, but more worried about my whereabouts. She called someone to let them know that I was back, and that I was safe. I didn't try to run away again because Mama said she would come back for us. I believed her. I just didn't know when. Later, I would speak with Buttercup about it. I was elated to tell her that I saw Mama, and that she was coming back for us. Though I'm really not sure if that gave Buttercup much comfort. It seemed as if sadness had started to get the best of her.

After a couple of months I finally tried to adjust to my new living arrangements. Ms. Garrett was a nice lady, and I was growing fond of her. She would "press" or straighten my hair like Grandma used to do, sending me to school looking really pretty. I was also able to speak to my sister more frequently. Sharing our experiences and making each other laugh was mostly what our conversation was about. Plus, we were still hoping hard to see Mama again.

One night while I was preparing for bed, the local news came on. I was in the midst of putting my scarf over my hair. I never paid much attention to the news, but the news anchor caught my attention when she said a 27-year-old woman was found dead, shot in the head. Suddenly I was glued to the television set, trying to make sure that it wasn't Mama. I slowly tied my scarf, watching as they wheeled the gurney from a house, then zipped up the body bag. Then the news anchor said: "Blanche Kennedy was found shot to death." It was my mama!

"Mamaaaaaa!" My legs went weak as I screamed for her in anguish. Ms. Garrett rushed in to see what was wrong. She held me in her arms, but I was inconsolable. I cried to the point of complete exhaustion. I remember lying in the bed as Ms. Garrett changed the blanket. The blanket she would put over me was big and fluffy, which brought me some comfort. But the pain of Mama's death left me confused and heartbroken. I drifted off to sleep with the thought: "Nobody is coming back for us now."

I sat through Mama's funeral numb as I cried. I remember all the seats being filled during the funeral. My two aunts, cousins, and a host of Mama's friends were present as well. I tried to remember the good times just like the man who was speaking said to do. But I could only remember Mama's last words before leaving that day: "Be a big girl till I come back for y'all." I cried harder because I still longed for her. Immediately after the funeral, I went back to the foster home with Ms. Garrett who had accompanied me.

3

Kept and Sheltered

AFTER MAMA WAS murdered I was moved to several foster homes. They were different children's homes and a farm. The farm was way out in the middle of nowhere. My two sisters would accompany me there. I found out that my baby brother and sister, who were kept together, would soon be adopted. However Bam, my oldest brother, continued to stay with his father and would soon fall victim to his environment.

I was confused by all of these fast-changing events as my sisters and I headed to the farm where we were told we would live for a while. This farm was being run by John and Michelle who were awesome people. We lived in a ranch-style house on the farm, which had a cabin-like feel. The house was big and very well furnished. The dining table was huge enough to seat ten or more people. Everybody helped one another. This was where I first learned how to set a table, tend to different animals, and how to pray more often. John and Michelle were devoted Christians who accepted children into their home from all walks of life. They owned horses, cows, chicken, pigs, etc. At first I was scared of the animals, but soon I began to enjoy them. There were about five other children there. My sisters and I were the only Black people on the farm, and it seemed like we were the only ones in the whole town.

The couple, although they were white, didn't recognize any

differences in our skin color. We were all treated the same. They also loved country music. The farm was the place where I learned my first country song. The couple prayed and spoke about God, which made me think of Grandma and how she prayed and kept us in church. Losing Mama was painful, but being with my sisters brought me comfort. We felt like we had finally arrived at a place that we could get used to—or so we thought.

But then the couple came to us one day to let us know that we would be leaving them. They explained that our stay with them was only temporary. The social worker found another place for us to go.

So the day soon came when we sadly left the farm. I remember that the car ride was very quiet. We had no choice but to accept the fact that nobody was ever coming to get us. Mama was gone. There was no home for us to go to, no one for us to call. All we had was each other, so we played the cards that we were dealt.

We pulled up to a very big building. My younger sister, Shaunta, was not able to stay at this particular place. It was a children's home, but she was sent to another orphanage because they didn't have space for her. Buttercup was sent to St. James, another children's home, while I stayed at the Annie Malone Children's Home where I was placed with the younger girls.

Annie Malone was a big part of the inner city community where I lived. Most of my days were spent defending and protecting myself from bullies. The staff took us on various outings such as concerts, the Rams football games, St. Louis Cardinal baseball games, to the theatre and opera, and to hear the symphony orchestra. You name it and we were able to experience it. We also attended the annual May Day Parade which was always fun and festive. Despite the fact that Annie Malone had all these different events to entertain us, I was still very saddened by Mama's death. Nothing would bring her back, and I was reminded constantly of this painful fact as I watched the other girls leave with their family members on weekends and holidays. I felt hurt, alone, and angry. At times I would just explode in a tantrum of crying and screaming. "I wanna leave this place!" I would shout as loud as I possibly could as I sat torturing myself with thoughts of all the years I might have to spend there.

Moreover, there were about six beds and six dressers in one very large room where I stayed. Most of the girls were gone for the weekend. So I stood at the bottom of my bed, staring at the barred window as I began to pray: *"God please send me a Mama. I wanna leave this place. Amen."* After I prayed, I instantly realized that there were fun activities planned for the weekend. One particular weekend the music group TLC came to visit us; however, Lisa Lopez or "Left Eye" was not with them. Music was my therapy. The members of the group were beautiful. They were also one of my favorite girl groups at the time. Their presence was a reminder for me to dream big and never give up on my dreams. I knew God was taking care of me even though I was ashamed of being an orphan.

A couple of years passed. One evening the social worker would pay me a visit. I was told that there were spots available at the orphanage where my little sister Shaunta was staying. She told me that Buttercup and I would be moving there with Shaunta. We were excited to be back together again. Within a couple of weeks, we would all be living at St. Vincent Home for Children. St. Vincent was a Catholic facility. Many nuns lived there and a couple of priests. This orphanage had long, white polished hallways, high ceilings, and a chapel. The whole place was very quiet and had a peaceful feel to it. I attended Sunday mass, though it was different from what I was accustomed to. However, I enjoyed it because I found peace in prayer and praying.

I was placed in the same apartment with my sister Shaunta, and Buttercup was placed in the older girls' apartment. I say "apartment" because there was a kitchen, a living room, and bathrooms. There was one very large carpeted bedroom that held eight beds and eight dressers. Plus, there was always something to do and places to go. There was a skating rink, swimming pool, auditorium, basketball court, gym, games, etc. We enjoyed the many outings and events available to us.

Christmas was filled with an abundance of toys. But most importantly, there was always someone praying for us. Mass was held every Sunday. They even had a school upstairs, and we wore uniforms to school daily. St. Vincent was a blessed and holy place. One night something strange happened. My bed was located by the window. Outside the window was a statue of an angel and a child. One night a fluorescent figure sat on the end of my bed. "Everything is going to be okay," the shining figure said to me. I wasn't scared or frightened. I just sat up and wiped my eyes to get a clear view. I looked around the dark room to see if anyone was awake to witness this experience, but everyone was sound asleep. I never spoke of it, not even to my sisters. I didn't want to chance being put on medication like some of the other girls.

We lived there for three years or so. Still, sometimes my sisters and I would have bouts of anger and sadness that would come over us. What do you do when no one is coming for you? When children don't know what to do or how to express their emotions, it will be displayed in their behavior. I found myself constantly defending myself as well

19

as my sisters. Not only from the children, but from a couple of staff members too. They would call my sister names such as "fat," saying that us Kennedy girls would never amount to anything. Though I knew this was a good place, there are times when not-so-good people end up there as well. I continued to wonder what would happen to my sisters and me. So I prayed: *"Dear God, I don't wanna be in this place. Please help me and my sisters. In the name of the Father, Son, and the Holy Spirit. Amen."*

4

Not By Coincidence

THE PRAYER WORKED because we left St. Vincent. My little sister Shaunta was sent to a foster home while Buttercup and I were sent to Echo Children's Home. As I settled in, a staff person told me it would be best to write my initials on the inside of my clothing because of possible theft.

"How do you pronounce your name?" the lady asked.

"Daphine," I replied.

"Do you have a nickname?" she inquired.

"No!" I replied, because I was ashamed of my nickname .

"I can't believe you don't have a nickname," she commented as she looked me over.

Oh, yes! I have a nickname," I said, suddenly changing my mind. "My nickname is Shay." I created this name out of thin air because I wanted to separate myself from everything that was happening to me. I knew I was an orphan, but I no longer wanted to remember the pain or events that had brought me here to this place. Daphine became the observer as Shay moved through life. Daphine was ashamed of the cards she was dealt, but Shay was her fearless alter ego. Shay had to go into survival mode.

Growing up, I had seen and heard a lot which made it easier for me to adapt to this environment. This place was very different, but Shay had no problem adapting. The kids were tougher and meaner, and so was Shay. The casual use of profanity and fights were common. I found myself getting into a couple of fights, using lots of profanity, and having plenty of arguments as well. Not by choice but only to defend myself. I was all about defending my property, myself, and my space. In this environment I learned how to hold my own.

While staying there I was allowed to go where the older girls were located to visit Buttercup from time to time. On my first visit, I saw a boy who was dressed in all red. He sat near the cottage where I was headed to visit Buttercup. His eyes focused on me as I neared the cottage.

"Where you going?" he said, with a little bass in his voice.

"None of your business!" I snapped at him. "You know you're not supposed to be over here on the girls' side," I said, giving him a laser stare as I examined his caramel face.

He repeated himself once more. "I said where you going?" the boy asked, demanding a response.

"I live here, Nosey," I sharply replied, not caring if he knew because I figured he lived here as well.

"I go to school here. This is where my bus comes to take me home," he fired back at me. "Plus, I sit where I wanna sit!" he added, obviously trying to get my attention. "You've got a smart mouth, but you're beautiful," he told me as he smiled and pulled back the red hoodie from his head, allowing me to see more of his handsome face.

"You go to the bad kids' school here on campus?" I asked, wondering what kind of mischief he was up to.

"Yeah," he said quickly with a serious look on his face that I

22

interpreted to mean: "Yeah, so what?"

Secretly liking his boldness and carefree manner, I shrugged my shoulders as I began walking towards the door to visit Buttercup. "If you wanna get out of here, my mama will come get you... you gonna have to go to church though because that's all my mama do. I have some sisters too," he added. He smiled and nodded while putting the hoodie back over his head like he already knew his plan for rescuing me would work for sure.

"I'm Ivan" he stood up as he spoke his name with confidence.

"I'm Shay," I said, rolling my eyes. I was puzzled by the way he was eyeing me as I entered the cottage.

"You know I'm gon be right here tomorrow!" he yelled just before I let the door slam behind me. Well, if this place ever gets to be intolerable, I might consider taking him up on his offer, I thought to myself.

"What took you so long?" Buttercup asked as I entered her room.

"I'm here now, so hush!" I replied, not wanting to tell her about the conversation between the strange boy Ivan and me. Buttercup and I shared our experiences, laughed, and joked. She too was having a hard time adjusting to this place. Buttercup was sweet and had a heart of gold. I looked up to her and loved her. We were close. She always had good advice and knew how to cheer me up. I already knew we shared the same pain, but now we shared the same thoughts. We missed Bam and our younger siblings tremendously. We didn't speak to Shaunta often or visit her much, but only heard that her behavior was getting out of control. There was nothing we could do to help one another.

"Sister, don't cry!" I said to Buttercup as I started crying. "One day we're gonna be grown, then we can be together and do whatever we want." Though I had no idea of what it meant to be grown, I figured grown-ups could do whatever they wanted. Plus, I wanted to reassure Buttercup that everything would be okay as soon as we were old enough to control our own lives—or so I thought.

"I can't take this place. I'm gonna run away, okay?" Buttercup said. She was letting me know not to be alarmed by her absence.

"Where to?" I asked.

"I don't know…somewhere away from here," she replied.

Our visit ended and I walked back to my living quarters saddened. On the way back I noticed a boy in handcuffs and shackles. I was baffled by what I was seeing, yet curious about why he was there. I stopped to ask him why he was there as the officer took off the handcuffs and shackles. "For truancy and skipping school," He answered. I walked away puzzled and confused. Had we done something wrong to end up here? I thought to myself.

Buttercup and I wanted out of this place. And so I prayed: *"Dear God, Buttercup and I are not happy here. We don't know what to do. God, please help us. In the name of The Father, Son, and The Holy Spirit. Amen."*

Though I was only twelve, I wanted to be an adult. I wanted a place to call my own. I wanted to be somewhere away from here. Buttercup did run away and was later found safe. She didn't return to Echo with me. Instead, she was sent to Boys and Girls Town, a distant place outside the city for youth who were at risk for running away. During this time I would see and hear from Bam more frequently. His father had met a nice lady who grew very fond of my brother. They moved in with Linda. She began to allow all of us to come over some weekends or holidays. She remained in my brother's life as a mother figure who supported him. Linda didn't have any children of her own, and us moving in or staying there on a regular basis was never mentioned.

We continued to stay in the children's home. One day a young lady came to visit me. I had never met her before, nor did I know who sent her to me. She just showed up one day. Her name was Ava. I'm sure the Echo staff knew who she was. This nice young lady grew to be very fond of me. She began taking me to different places to hang out, buying me clothes, talking to me, etc. Not long after, Ava asked her mother if I could live with them. Ava's mom already had other foster children living with her, so I asked Ava if there was any way possible that my sister Buttercup could come, too.

Her mom said yes, and my sister was able to join me. God will send people who you may not know to assist you while you are on this journey. I like to call these people "angels." On the way to our new foster home I noticed the neighborhood was different. We were no longer in the inner city. We were now in St. Louis County, in a middle class neighborhood. Manicured lawns, beautiful trees, and recycling bins were noticeable as we headed toward this new place.

As it turned out, the family was somewhat conservative. There were also rules to be followed. No going in the refrigerator and no cooking or making your own food. And you had to ask permission to use the phone. We slept and entertained ourselves downstairs mostly, which was more spacious. Ava made the stay there more welcoming. Although her mom was our official guardian, it seemed as if Ava was the one in charge. We went to school every day and tried to make the best of our circumstances.

We didn't converse or connect with Ava's mom much. She rarely talked to us, nor do I remember having many conversations with her. However, she did interact and communicate with her biological children. Ava was in her early twenties, and her younger sister was a teenager. I enjoyed Ava's companionship because she was like a big sister to me, but Buttercup was not happy.

"Do you like it here?" I asked.

"No!" she replied as she rolled her eyes. "You?" she asked.

"It's okay," I said, shrugging my shoulders. I knew exactly how Buttercup felt. I felt the same way at times. When you are a foster child in a home where there are biological children, you may notice that you are not treated the same. They may be allowed to go places and do certain things that a foster child may not. Still, I wanted to make the best out of this situation, despite the circumstances. Besides, I liked Ava and I was tired of moving. I also liked the school. I was a good student with grades to match.

Meanwhile the loss of Mama continued to pull Buttercup deeper into a well of sadness. I noticed the sadness in her eyes, and naturally I thought one of my silly jokes would cheer her up. "Want some ant cereal? I got some ant cereal for yah." I said, making a funny face and starting to laugh. But my jokes no longer helped. Buttercup was not laughing. Instead, tears fell from her eyes.

"I can't stay here," she said.

Buttercup ran away from this place, too. I knew she was hurting because of all we had been through. And I really didn't want to be apart from her. "Buttercup, please don't. They'll send you away if you run," I said. But my pleas fell on deaf ears. During that same time my little sister Shaunta continued to struggle with her placement. I'm sure she felt just as alone as we did. There just wasn't any foster homes that could take all of us. What was worst was that we would only get to visit each other very rarely. Afterwards, we would depart in sadness.

As for me, I did my best to follow my big sister. She was the one who always looked out for us back when Mama would leave us alone. She was the one who took on the responsibility of the mother role. Before leaving us alone, Mama would say, "Buttercup, you in charge till I get back." I even remember being furious with Buttercup because I wanted to be in charge. Soon as Mama would walk out the door, I'd say to Buttercup, "You not in charge of me, Lil girl. You just a tattletale!" Then we'd go tit for tat with one another, battling to get the last word in until we stumbled upon some laughter.

Buttercup was hurting and I knew it was my turn to look after her. So I asked the social worker if I could join her at the foster home where she was staying. My request was approved, and not by coincidence. Days later I left Ava's house to join Buttercup. After witnessing the pain in my sister's eyes, I had become very angry and resentful. I started blaming Mama for everything we had to endure. Even though she was gone, I was furious about the silence of her voice even in death. I buried my own pain in the hope that my sister's pain would subside.

I sure was happy to be back with Buttercup though. She knew me and understood me. I knew her pain and she knew mine. Still, I couldn't feel the depth of her pain and she couldn't feel mine. Therefore, I did my very best to mask my pain whenever I was around her. However, while living here we would have to go to daycare. Yes, that's right, a daycare. I couldn't believe it. A daycare was the last place I wanted to be. I was twelve years old and going to daycare. The daycare accepted children up to age thirteen.

Just the thought of attending daycare fueled me with frustration. Buttercup did not have to deal with this issue because she decided that she did not like this foster home either and would run away from this placement as well. She mostly ran to places in the city where my brother hung out. I felt relieved about that because Bam always looked out for us. He was our protector.

Like all of us, our big brother had a great sense of humor. If there was one thing we knew it was how to turn pain into laughter. But most importantly, I knew he would get Buttercup to turn herself in. He did not want her to be exposed to the type of environment he was in. He was a hustler now, even though he got a job after graduating from high school. I guess it wasn't paying enough because he soon started selling crack cocaine. It was really ironic since that was the very thing that destroyed Mama. Now it had manifested into my brother's life as well. Another thing was that Linda, his step mother, had raised him well. I guess he resorted to hustling in order to get the things he wanted in a much faster way.

Bam convinced Buttercup to turn herself in. After that she was sent to Epworth Children's Home. I never ran away with Buttercup because I thought I might end up in a worse place or situation. It was around this time that I stopped praying. I also stopped asking God for help because I thought maybe he had forgotten about us.

5

Everything Happens For A Reason

I DID NOT enjoy my new foster home. What I disliked most about it was living apart from Buttercup again. My days were filled with anger and frustration, but I kept my emotions hidden from the people around me. I went along with the daily routine even though I knew my anger and negative attitude was masking the tragic story I had been living through for years.

I longed for adulthood and often daydreamed about the life I wanted for myself. I wanted to put everything that had to do with foster homes, orphanages, and social workers behind me. But at the time I had to adjust my attitude in order to fit in. There was no other option. In addition, there was another foster child who lived at the house, including the foster parent's adopted daughter. I knew I wouldn't stay in this place long after she introduced the two girls to me. "Here are my two light-skinned daughters with long curly hair, and we are just gonna call you our chocolate baby," she said. I stood there speechless as she pointed out our differences in skin color and hair texture as if that really mattered.

Soon I began attending the daycare before and after school, and whenever school was out. My first day there I met the owner who would also be tending to all the children who came. She was beautiful, charismatic, and full of life. She was the happiest person I had ever met. She was so happy that I wondered what was wrong with her. She was also energetic and enthusiastic. Her personality shone bigger than the sun. Immediately I was drawn to her.

Her name was Angela Bryant. She spoke fast, but most importantly she loved children. She was known to the children as well as the community as "Ms. A." I was somewhat taken aback by her level of excitement because I had just arrived there. She squeezed my cheek and took my hand in hers. "What's wrong, baby girl?" she asked. "You're gonna love it here!"

I managed to let out a little smirk. It was like she had known me forever. That's a strange lady, I thought to myself as I filled my mouth with hot, buttery waffles. I began to enjoy the daycare. I could always look forward to fun, a hot meal, and an abundance of love at this daycare center which was called Kidz-N-Motion. The outside of the daycare was painted a bright pink and blue, with Mickey and Minnie Mouse on the front. There were plenty of toys, games, arts and crafts, etc. The daycare was not so bad after all. In fact, when it was time to leave, a sense of sadness slowly crept over me. But Ms. A instantly noticed my change in mood. She came over to me and kneeled down, saying, "It's gonna be okay, baby girl." I gave her a blank stare because life—as I knew it—was not okay.

The foster home lady arrived to pick us up. As I got into the vehicle Ms. A ran outside and yelled: "Don't worry! Tomorrow we have ice skating and a picnic!" Then she did a cartwheel right there on the spot. "Wow!" I said to myself as I raised an eyebrow in amazement.

I wanted to stay at the daycare instead of returning to my foster home. And deep down inside, I wished I could lived with the day care lady. I knew she loved children, but most of all she understood children. There I was in deep thought again, wishing I was someplace other than where I was.

I had to admit that I was not happy at this foster home. The skin color comments had persisted, and I just didn't want to stay there anymore. However, I became close friends with the other foster child, Paris, during my stay there. We decided to say we were cousins if anybody asked. This was to avoid the suspicion of being a foster child. Plus, I didn't look anything like her or the other girl who lived there. It worked, too.

We shared childhood stories as well as secrets. She also had a good sense of humor, which I enjoyed. It was like having another sister. Though I enjoyed the daycare, I knew I wouldn't be in that situation long because of the constant comments about color, along with being treated differently. However, I didn't have a clue about where I would go or end up. I needed someone to talk to about my experience at this home. The first person that came to mind was Ava. She always had good advice, and maybe she could help get me out of this place.

One day I called Ava and expressed my unhappiness about where I was living. She informed me that her grandmother was now a foster parent, and if I wanted to, I could live with her. I made a call to my social worker to discuss my desire to move — and it was approved.

Shortly afterwards, I moved in with Ava's grandmother, Ms. Vera. I figured this foster home would be better than the others. Plus, I would get to hang out with Ava sometimes. Ms. Vera was a church-going lady with old-fashioned values. However, I already knew that going to church would be essential to my stay here. At the same time I was still filled with so much anger and resentment towards Mama and being separated from my siblings. Anyone who crossed me would be sure to feel the hurt that I hid deep inside.

I missed my siblings more and more each day, while I seemed to hear from them less and less. I would visit them occasionally, depending on our good behavior or if the social worker was available to facilitate the visits. I also stayed in touch with my "friend-cousin" Paris by phone during my stay there. And not just her, I also secretly stayed in touch with the boy who was escorted to Echo Children's Home in handcuffs and shackles.

Yes, I was young, naive, and curious. I wanted to know more about him and his life. He was from the hood. I was 14 and he was 16 years old. Leon was easy on the eyes, dressed well, had a car, and he had that "bad boy" edge to him that I liked due to being raised in the hood. He became my best friend as well as my boyfriend. He understood me and my circumstances, and never judged. Leon could relate to me because he too came from a broken home. Also, his mother had once struggled with addiction and his father was absent from his life. He was being raised by his grandmother. Our similar backgrounds helped us to form a tight bond. In addition, he was street savvy and had transportation. At that point in my life I knew he would be beneficial. I figured he could help navigate me out of situations I didn't want to be in. In my own brokenness, I'd attracted another broken soul.

I kept the communication between Leon and me secret from Ms. Vera and Ava. I only shared my secret with Paris and Buttercup. I had chosen to live with Ms. Vera, whom I'd never met before, because I thought surely Ava wouldn't recommend that I live there if this was a bad place. But I grew to like Ms. Vera who had a deep and profound love for God. She read the Bible daily and could be heard throughout the house singing hymns. We went to church constantly, on weekends and weekdays.

I enjoyed going to church because Grandma Rose instilled that in me. But Grandma only made us go on Sundays. Here I went to church so often that I would even sit through funeral services of church members whom I didn't even know. Going to church so much began to agitate me. I loved God and had learned how to pray to Him. God had even answered my prayers when I was in places I didn't want to be. But I still wondered why God had not answered my most important prayer when I lived at the Annie Malone orphanage. I'd never forgotten my unanswered prayer: "God, please send me a Mama." Had God forgotten about me and my siblings? This saddened me.

I just wanted to be a normal teen with a normal life. But instead I was here with Ms. Vera who had God all around her. Gospel music played daily in the house, and even in the car. She sang gospel hymns and read the word of God day in and day out. And here I was still waiting on God's help! Ms. Vera was steadfast in her beliefs about church and God. There was absolutely no way of getting around going to church.

On Sunday mornings, I eagerly waited for her to put on her church hat. She owned a plethora of church hats and they were all beautiful. She had all shapes, sizes, and colors. She dressed well for church, putting on her Sunday's best. Whenever she would leave the house and forget her hat, I'd remind her by saying, "Ms. Vera...your hat?" Then I'd giggle because she reminded me of the elder mothers who sat in the front row at the church where Grandma used to send us. During service I would sit there thinking about my life, only to be interrupted by one of the elder deacons singing, "I love the Lord, He heard my cry." Was the deacon letting me know that God could hear my cry for help? I didn't know. So I usually couldn't wait for service to end.

6

God Answers Prayers

AFTER CHURCH SERVICE I ate Sunday dinner and did my chores. I hurried through the chores because only then would I be able to get on the phone. I called Paris to talk about how overwhelmed I was with so much church, and how I wanted to leave but had no place to go. That's when she told me that she no longer lived at her last foster home. She now lived with Ms. A.

"The daycare lady!" I said with excitement.

"You can come here with me," Paris said.

"I may run away," I told her. I immediately began thinking about who would pick me up. Asking Bam was out of the question. He wouldn't assist me because he always wanted me to do the right thing. Leon would question my plan, but I knew he would come.

"First, I have to call Leon to see if he can pick me up and drop me off there," I told Paris.

"Be sure to pack your bag," she replied.

"Okay," I said.

All at once I became very nervous about making the decision to run away. The last time I ran away it was to find Mama. But this time it was to be with the happy lady who loved children. But what was I going to say to Ms. Vera? I thought to myself. I couldn't tell her there was too much God at her house for me to handle, and that I wanted to leave because of it. My reasoning sounded like nonsense even to me. Just imagine that! Too much God!!

But still I was determined to leave. I made up my mind to leave without giving her notice about my plans. I did not go about this the right way, but I really wanted to see what life would be like if I went to live with the daycare lady. Then I made a call to Leon to discuss my plan so that he would be there to pick me up. He was always down for whatever, and I knew I could depend on him. It was nighttime already, and I told him to let the phone ring once, then hang up. That would be our signal.

My bag was packed. The time to execute my plan was now. My heart pounded with nervousness since I didn't know what to expect from either Ms. Vera or Ms. A. Thoughts of consequences for my actions raced through my head. Then the phone rang once. My racing thoughts stopped. The palms of my hands were sweating as I reached for my bag. I looked straight ahead as I walked toward the front door. My mind was made up and there was no turning back. As I headed down the stairs, I glanced over into Ms. Vera's room. My eyes locked with hers as she carried on doing what she was doing. She didn't utter one word nor try to stop me. She just let me be. It was like a scene from a movie when a child ventures out into the world to see what lies ahead. I was free to go.

I finally reached my destination. Paris greeted me at the door. There was a full house of people there already. Ms. A had four children of her own, Paris, and a friend who lived there as well. When I walked in the door she immediately recognized me. She was excited to see me, but appeared somewhat baffled.

"What are you doing out so late?" she asked me.

"She ran away. Is it okay if she stay here with us?" Paris interjected before I could get any words out.

"Oh no!" Ms. A replied. "The lady will report you as a runaway, and I will be in big trouble if you stay here." I was speechless as I began thinking about my next move and where I could go. Then Ms. A said, "I'm gonna call your social worker first thing in the morning. If she approves, then you can stay."

"See…I told you," Paris said. I was instantly filled with joy and gratitude as a big smile spread across my face.

"Thank you, Ms. A," I said to her. "Thank you, Jesus!" I softly whispered to myself. I couldn't believe it because I was exactly where I wanted to be. I anxiously waited to hear whether or not this would be my new home. And sure enough, the social worker gave her approval for Ms. A to become my new foster parent. I had no problems adjusting. There were only a few house rules, which were to dress appropriately, follow curfew, and to make sure that my whereabouts were known. I had no problem following these rules.

Ms. A was known for her love for children, her work ethic, and her philanthropy. Being of service to others was one of the many things I admired about her. Ms. A seemed to have boundless energy. She provided job opportunities, generously donated money to those in need, gave a helping hand to the less fortunate, opened her home to youth, and shared her business knowledge with other entrepreneurs. In addition, she also found time to visit homeless shelters where she would speak to teenage mothers. She would even allow me to accompany her sometimes.

Ms. A worked early mornings, late evenings, and at times late into the night, getting little or no sleep. Her giving spirit and hard work paid off because her businesses grew rapidly, catapulting her to success. She was very ambitious. Instead of one daycare, she now owned five. She was filled with determination and wore many hats as a woman. She inspired me and I admired her. Not only was she a single mother of four children, but it was as if God whispered to her: "Here's another child. Guide her, love her, and show her the way."

And that she did. While living with Ms. A, I was able to be myself. She allowed me to express my feelings and thoughts without consequences or fear of punishment. Though I was still very negative at times and held on tight to my anger and resentment towards Mama, she never mentioned my attitude. I didn't understand why, but she would only acknowledge my positive behavior. Yes, there were times when I made poor decisions or made inappropriate remarks. Yet she never spoke to me about my negative attitude. However, when I behaved in such a manner, she would respond: "You hurt me when you said that." Or she might say: "You hurt me when you did that." It was words like those that caused me to see the anger and negativity I was displaying. I didn't want to disappoint her, and surely not hurt her. So I tried very hard to bury those negative emotions. At times to no avail.

Ms. A played a phenomenal role in my life. Whenever she had a big project or task to complete she would say, "I can do anything I put my mind to." She would say this with excitement and conviction. Then she would say, "Repeat after me baby girl, say: I can! I will! and I am!" I would repeat after her without conviction. I can remember not wanting to be bothered with her daycare slogans. Instead, I sat there listening vaguely, wondering if my sisters were okay.

I hadn't spoken to Buttercup since I left Ms. Vera's house. Guilt began to set in because I wanted my sisters to share this same experience of being with someone who cared about them. Nobody's gonna take all of us, I said to myself. Plus, Buttercup and I were both teenagers. Time after time I would say to myself: "Soon I'm gonna be on my own, and I'm gonna have my own place." Although I was where I wanted to be—living with Ms. A who accepted me as I was—I felt powerless separated from all of my siblings.

However, the day came when I finally spoke to Buttercup on the phone. "Buttercup!" I said with excitement. We both giggled and burst into laughter. Laughter always connected us. It was our way of communicating with one another. For us, laughter was the emotion we used to express family love. Even without using words, we knew each of us was okay when we shared laughter.

"Where are you?" I asked.

"Girl, you would not believe this house and these cars! I'm in Lake St. Louis."

I had never even heard of Lake St. Louis, let alone where it was located. She went on and on about how big and beautifully furnished the house was as I listened in amazement.

"Do you like it there, sister?" I asked.

"Yes! It's just boring out here," she replied. "Where you at?" she asked.

"I live with the daycare lady now," I said with a smile.

"I just don't see how you can go to a daycare every day with yo' big ole self. Ooouuwee!" she replied in disbelief. Both of us burst out laughing.

"Buttercup…guess what?" I said.

"Girl what?" she asked anxiously.

"I gotta tell you something…you not gonna believe this," I said.

"Hurry up and tell me," she replied with frustration.

"I live in a big, beautiful house in the suburbs too, Buttercup."

Our conversation ended with us both being happy for one another and thankful to have such a great experience. However, we were still unhappy being apart. Have you ever been thankful to be in a place, yet unhappy in that very same place? Well, truth is, you can't be thankful and unhappy at the same time. Please learn how to trust God's plan as well as the journey you might have to take through difficult times, because it may just be a blessing in disguise. Even though we couldn't be together, I felt better because Buttercup had met someone whom she spoke very highly of and who loved her. She too had met a mother figure. But most importantly, she was not talking about running away.

As for my little sister Shaunta, she too made a connection with a mother figure before leaving the orphanage. She told me about a lady who came to St. Vincent Children's Home one day to sell hand-made jewelry. Shaunta had received an allowance from the orphanage for good behavior and completion of her chores, so she used some of her money to make a purchase from the lady. She was surprised the next day when this lady called the orphanage and asked permission to be her mentor.

Although Shaunta did not live with this lady (her angel), she became an important part of her life from that day. My little sister's new mentoring angel remained in her life over the years, never leaving her side as Shaunta worked through her anger and frustration issues. This nice lady eventually purchased some land. She then had a big beautiful three-story home built on her property. This gorgeous, custom-designed home was exquisitely crafted to her taste, with a wrap-around deck, vaulted ceilings, etc. And the lake on the property was just God showing out!

Being exposed to a better environment and a different way of living was a blessing to us from God. I was grateful and overjoyed that my little sister was able to share this experience as well. This was my confirmation that God does answer prayers in His own divine timing. You see, I never asked God to give my sisters a mother figure when I was a little girl because I was always told that nobody would take in all of us. Surely God had taken all of us in!

7

You Get What You Ask For

I WISH I could say that life went well for us from that moment on. I continued to do well at school and at the daycare. I had everything a teenager could ask for, but I still felt as if something was missing. It seemed as if I was searching for something. Maybe somewhat aimlessly, yet determined to find it. One day while working at the daycare I took a break from my duties just to observe the way Ms. A was able to multi-task.

"Hey baby girl, everything okay?" she called out to me.

"Yes!" I replied with uncertainty.

"What do you want out of life?" she asked as she stopped everything she was doing.

I shrugged my shoulders. "I'm not sure yet," I replied. I just want to be on my own, in my own place, I thought to myself.

"You know you can do and become whatever you want, right?"

She went on. "You see there's nothing I can't do. Everything I touch turns to gold!" she said with excitement and conviction. "Go to college. But for now go around the daycare to make sure that all the restrooms are clean," she added.

As I was cleaning the restrooms I briefly thought about college and how Ms. A's college degree had nothing to do with childcare. Her degree was in electrical engineering. Ms. A later confided to me that her idea about starting a daycare came to her when no one would keep all of her children while she worked. I also thought about how, despite the many challenges she had to face growing up, somehow she'd still managed to become very successful. So I figured I would worry about college later. And besides, I still had a few more years of high school to complete.

I continued to learn the daycare business as I worked there. At times I'd notice that a few of the children were dirty, unkempt, and really hungry. "Why are these children not properly cared for?" I asked Ms. A with frustration. Though I was really hoping I would get an answer as to why I and my siblings were not properly cared for. "Well, maybe it's because her mother was never a mother to her, and she simply doesn't know how. That's why I'm gonna help teach, guide, assist, and talk to her. It's really not her fault," Ms. A said. Then she would send a daycare worker to the store to purchase diapers, clothes, and shoes if need be.

It was at that very moment that I forgave Mama, because with her addiction she simply didn't know how to care for us. Mama was wounded and broken, and I understood that in that condition she was not able to cope with reality, nor even take care of herself. This made it impossible for her to look after us properly. Later, I felt a strong need to express my feelings aloud to Blanche: "Mama I forgive you. I truly forgive you. You simply didn't know how to care for us in your addiction and in your condition. You did the best you could, Mama. I forgive you, Mama," I said as I wept tears that were long overdue.

Not long after, I grew tired of the daycare center and began to rebel. Life for me had become so routine, so mundane. I wanted to be free. I no longer wanted to adhere to any rules or curfew. I wanted to do things my way. As a teen I had sneaky ways, especially when it came to bad boys. Not only had I kept in contact with Leon, I'd also kept in contact with the other boy I met at Echo named Ivan. I didn't see Ivan often because he lived the fast life. So this particular weekend I lied to Ms. A, asking if I could stay over at my friend's house. Truth is, Ivan had sisters around my age, and I was allowed to go for that reason.

I'd decided to take Ivan up on his offer from years ago. Meanwhile I told Ms. A. that I had a ride back, a lie I told her with uncertainty. I got a ride to Ivan's house from a friend of Ms. A who worked at the daycare. I was supposed to be home by midnight on this particular Saturday, but neither Ivan nor I had a way of getting me back home. As midnight approached, I called Ms. A to let her know I couldn't find a ride. She was upset and disappointed with me. "Oh my goodness Shay," she said. "You told me you had a ride home! Now you're gonna have to stay there until the afternoon sometime because I have some things to do. I can't believe this!" she went on scolding me.

Well, it was Sunday morning now. And remember that nothing just happens. Just as Ivan had told me years ago, I had to go to church with the family. Thing is, I was inappropriately dressed in Daisy Dukes (really short shorts) and a belly shirt, breaking another one of Ms. A's rules. Nor did Ivan's mother know that I had stayed the night in his room. Moreover, she instantly became furious with him after finding out that I had done so. "She's just gonna have to wear what she has on!" she said. "I'm not gonna be late for service!" She was steadfast about church also, and no one was allowed to stay back from going, including me. I couldn't fit in either of his sister's clothes. Frantic, I raced back to the phone to call Ms. A., hoping she could possibly postpone her plans in order to prevent the level of embarrassment I was about to endure. Yes, I was a selfish teenager.

There's an old saying that came to my mind. "You make the bed; you lie in it." Please be mindful of the choices you make. For every action there's an equal and opposite reaction. Because of my poor decision making, I'd created a situation for myself with no way out. "Everybody go get in the van now!" Ivan's mother demanded. We soon arrived at church. Immediately, I could feel the stares and whispers as I headed toward my seat. I sat down stiff as a statue, looking straight ahead to avoid any eye contact from church members.

I was not even conscious of my actions back then. I sat through the entire service without ever asking for forgiveness for my lies and disobedience. And so I did the only thing I knew to do at that moment. I prayed: *"It's me again Father… help me, Lord. I really messed up this time. Amen."* I said all this to myself as I clasped both palms together, making praying hands. Soon afterwards, I began looking around, no longer feeling ashamed nor embarrassed as the Divine Spirit within me spoke: **"Come as you are, for you are my child. I accept you just as you are."** Church members, let's not shun nor turn our children away, for they may very well be just as broken and wounded as I was at that time.

Due to my choices and continuous rebellion, however, my stay with Ms. A came to an end. "Baby girl, I love you and I will always be here for you. You know you can always call me if you need anything," she said to me as we parted ways.

"Okay," I replied nonchalantly. Desperate for change, I wanted my life to unfold now. I was fearless even though I was uncertain about what lay ahead. Some days later, I was taken to Evangelical Children's Home. This was a gated place with a campus-like feel to it. There was one main building in the center of the campus with two or three smaller cottages on each side. "Oh God! Not this again!" I thought to myself. Moments later I was introduced to Mr. Harris who was responsible for the intake of new residents. He immediately noticed my attitude and how eager I was to get the process over with. "Hello, Ms. Kennedy," he spoke to me. "I've heard that you want to start the path of independent living. I want to assure you that you are in the right place because we have a transitional living program to assist you towards that goal. You will not be staying here on this campus. Instead, we have a house located in the community where you will live."

"Do you know how long I will have to live there before I can be placed in independent living?" I asked.

"Well, Ms. Kennedy, that's up to you. However, I believe you will do exceptionally well," he said.

Just as my social worker and I were leaving his office, he remarked: "Ms. Kennedy, there's something about you…you're going to grow up and do great things. When you turn 21, come back and I'll employ you."

"Okay," I replied nonchalantly. After leaving Mr. Harris's office, I thought again about his gesture of offering me employment, which was very kind. But surely he had to be out of his mind to think I'd be willing to return. "Once I leave this place I'm moving on with my life. Why would I come back here?" I ranted to myself as I shook my head.

Shortly after, the social worker and I drove to the transitional living house where I would be staying. When I walked in, the house had a welcoming and homey feel to it. As I settled in, I went over the rules and my responsibilities as a resident. I was determined to do everything that was required of me in order to hasten the day when I would be on my own.

I was determined to be reunited with my sisters, and I thought that once I was on my own, nobody would get in the way of us seeing each other or being together. But there's an old saying: "If you ever want to make God laugh, tell Him your plans." A few days later I tried contacting Buttercup. Apparently, the suburban life had become too boring for my big sister because I was informed that she no longer lived in Lake St. Louis. I was told that Buttercup now lived at Villa Maria, a residential home for pregnant teens. I was shocked to find out that Buttercup was pregnant. Not with one baby, but twins.

At age 17, after giving birth to my nephews, Buttercup decided to move in with her children's father. Around the same time I was headed to another placement after meeting the requirements for the Evangelical Children's Home transitional living program. I was so elated to find out I had been approved for independent living. Within a couple of weeks I was taken to Marygrove Children's Home. This was a Catholic facility where nuns also lived. And again, this children's home was campus-like and gated, with several smaller cottages. I was notified by the intake worker that the nuns would be praying for me daily. That brought me comfort though I didn't know what to expect.

"Is this where I'll be living?" I asked the social worker. She informed me that the independent living apartments were located throughout the community. I remember feeling relieved that the apartment wasn't located on the campus. Even up to that time I was still ashamed and embarrassed about having to live in such places. It was like they not only branded me as an orphan, but they broadcast to the world the path my siblings and I had traveled to get where we were. I never spoke of any foster homes or orphanages to anyone. Mostly, I'd avoid any questions pertaining to my childhood in an effort to hide painful events and memories. I was unconsciously blind to the blessings my life was offering me.

I was now on my own, in my own place, just as I believed I would be. Only without my sisters. I was there alone, and immediately informed that no one else was permitted to live there. This program was supposed to be a stepping stone to prepare me for adulthood. I was responsible for making it to school on my own, for following the rules as a tenant, and finding part-time employment. I gladly complied with all rules and expectations because this was what I'd been longing for.

Still, things had not turned out exactly as I'd planned, an outcome that taught me to look for the lesson in every situation. Finally, I had to let go of my own preconceived notions of how I wanted my life to unfold. You see, I was trying to control God's plan for my life. I'd even made plans for my sister to join me, without ever asking her what she wanted. Nor did I know she would become a mother. I just assumed that we would be together once I was on my own and in my own place.

I didn't have any financial responsibility for the apartment. Therefore, it was not mine, technically. Truth is, because my heart and mind was set on my own plan rather than surrendering control to God's plan, I felt disappointed and defeated. In addition, I was still hiding my truth from myself. I continued to use the alias I'd created for myself (Shay). In doing this, I'd created a negative ego or self-image due to my past hurt and pain. Though I had forgiven Mama, I just didn't understand why I had to endure all that I had gone through. Subconsciously, I didn't know I'd created a shield, an armor of protection that I was using in order to hide the pain I truly felt. Hiding the pain made it easy to hide from my past. I would even dress the pain up with clothes to my liking, a flawless hair style, and a beautiful fake smile to match. Blinded to the blessings strewn along my path, it was like I was wearing camouflage. I'd blended in perfectly with a society filled with other "pain bodies" and secret keepers who were also aimlessly searching for their life's purpose as well.

I bet you're wondering right now: "Did you ever get what you asked for?" The answer is no. You only get what you believe you will receive, believing that you have already received. And I really wasn't sure about what I wanted once I discovered that my sister was a young mother of two children. Yes, I believed I would be on my own and in my own place. And I wanted my sister with me. It is my opinion that one cannot will or want something for anyone else. It is solely up to that person what he or she wants for their own life. God gives us free will to choose. God's plan for each person is different. I soon found out that Buttercup didn't want to live in the county the way I had imagined it. In fact, she found that living in the county was very boring . She really enjoyed the hustle and bustle of city living at the time. It was in that moment that I discovered that you don't get what you ask for. You only get what you believe you will receive for yourself, believing that you have already received!

8

Re-routed

DURING THE RIDE in search of my new apartment, the social worker informed me that I had several selections to choose from. As we pulled up to the first apartment, I realized that the area was familiar to me. I was immediately drawn to the apartments after noticing how well-kept they were. After the tour, I knew that this one special apartment would be my choice. It was very spacious, with a balcony and a pool. In addition to these amenities, the apartment was in the same school district I'd attended when I lived with Ms. A. I would be living just a few miles from the daycare center.

After submitting the application, I was immediately given the key because of the contract the owners had with Marygrove Children's Home. Within a few days the furniture was delivered, and I was able to settle in. I remember being very thankful that I'd finally reached the destination I'd been yearning for. During this time I was able to see Buttercup and Bam more often. By then Shaunta had left the orphanage and was now in a foster home. It wasn't long after that I found out she was pregnant at 14 years old, and had been moved to Villa Maria Home for pregnant teens. Thankfully, she was allowed to come visit me on some occasions.

Life for my siblings and I was constantly changing. I had become accustomed to change. So I began adjusting to life as I knew it and being on my own. I was learning fast how to become more independent. After finding employment at several local fast food restaurants, I'd decided that I would much rather work at the daycare. After a few weeks of thinking about it, I'd mustered up enough courage to ask Ms. A if I could come back and work. Proud of the progress I'd made, Ms. A allowed me to work at the daycare. Being in charge of my own life plus my newfound independence was just what I'd been waiting to accomplish.

I continued to do well in school. I had more than enough credits to graduate. This situation prompted me to write a letter to the principal asking if I could be relieved of my classes pending graduation. That request was also approved, and I was still able to participate in the graduation ceremony. Things were headed in the right direction for me. And even though Buttercup didn't enjoy living in the county, she still made time to come visit me. This particular day she came with all sorts of notebooks and folders filled with poems, as well as a host of positive quotations and affirmations. To my surprise, she had written lots of short stories and poems.

Her poems were really well-written to me because some of them would make me smile, laugh out loud, and even weep. I enjoyed the precious moments we shared together. Yet I was baffled by her hidden talent as I thumbed through notebook after notebook of her work. From then on, whenever she would visit me, she would bring me a book. Even for my birthday, I'd receive a book. I remember putting each book away immediately since I wasn't interested at all.

"How 'bout giving me a shirt or pair of sandals?" I would ask her. "Did either of those items ever cross your mind?"

I said that hoping she would get the message and stop bringing me books. "Girl read the books. You're gonna love them!" she'd always say. Then we would both giggle and bust out laughing.

I never made a big fuss about Buttercup hiding her talent because by now I realized that I'd managed to hide in plain sight, too. You see, I thought that all of the painful events in my past defined me. There seemed to be no escape as I played these events over in my mind. This mental rehearsal continued even as I grew older. I told myself I was a child of a drug addict. And because of that I'd been labeled as an orphan in a system that separated me from my siblings. I felt abandoned and completely ashamed of my life. I couldn't understand why I had been given such a life of deprivation.

It was these thoughts that had me confused. I moved through life searching for who I was. Please be mindful of the story that you tell yourself. You are not your experience. Know that life's circumstances are only experiences. Therefore, learn to look for the lesson in all things. Adversity shapes and molds you for your life's purpose. Adversity, however painful or difficult, puts you on a journey to help those whom God has called you to serve. Which is why I was re-routed. Re-routed back to my second mother (Ms. A) whom God had entrusted with my life in the absence of my biological mother.

Since I sort of considered myself grown now, I figured I could have things my way, an attitude which caused me to go against the rules I'd signed up for. I allowed my boyfriend Leon to join me at the apartment. I made the decision because I was really lonely at the time. If I knew then what I know now, I would've known better than to mistake boredom for loneliness. How many of you out there know that I was never alone? Do you know why? Because "I Am" (God) was (is) always with me!

Back then I was still unconscious of my decision-making process. I was broken inside and so was Leon. I was clueless about love and completely lacked self-love, and so did he. It didn't take long for me to find myself going through "love motions" with a boy as full of past hurts and anger as I was. At the time I had no idea that I would soon have to pay the cost for all that he had endured. Things started out just fine, as it always does. Leon was there by my side, even attending my high school graduation ceremony, watching me walk across the stage to receive my diploma. I thought that his company would somehow fill the void I felt inside. During the first year we lived together, things were normal. Though I'd never personally seen what normal looks like, I tried to create my own normal.

God gives us free will, remember? So by the age of 19, I was pregnant. I knew that within a couple of years I would no longer be a ward of the state. I would be too old. Which is why I decided that it would be best for me to start preparing for the process of "aging out." I wanted to be settled somewhere before I gave birth to my daughter. I spoke to Ms. A about the transition I wanted to make because she had property that was not being utilized. This property was the very first daycare center I'd attended back when I was 12 years old. It was a single family home that had been turned into a daycare. Ms. A. allowed me to move in. Yes, it's safe to say that I was being re-routed by my Father—God—and yet I had no clue.

The daycare was still brightly painted pink and blue on the outside and Mickey and Minnie Mouse's shining faces would greet you should you knock on the door. I was thankful for a heart such as Ms. A's—God's angel—who poured her love upon me just at the critical moment that I needed guidance in my life. And though she was a sweet and loving mother figure, she showed me tough love as well.

"Now baby girl, you know I can't help you as long as you have a man living with you. The rent here is $600 dollars, and it's due on the first of each month," she said.

"Yes, I know that," I replied as I thought about the average checks I received from working at the daycare. Leon didn't have steady employment during this time. He would work temporary jobs, fix cars, or hustle marijuana. In my naïve mind and brokenness, I was not ready to let him go regardless of his many shortcomings. And besides, I figured we could manage to take care of our household—or at least I would!

Leon was happy, but I was confused. Leon nor I was equipped emotionally or financially as we welcomed my baby girl into the world. After my daughter was born, Leon seemed to consume alcohol even more frequently than before. Soon I would see how broken he really was as he inflicted his pain on me. Soon I had become numb to the verbal abuse I endured from him. Somewhere along the way, I lost the best friend I ever thought I had.

"Bitch, you ugly!" he once said to me. When he was drunk he threw insults, belittling comments, and hurtful remarks from his mouth like darts. Though I knew I wasn't ugly, my spirit was being torn down by the onslaught of verbal abuse. Eventually, his degrading comments and name calling made me feel very insecure. I thought about my dark skin, reflecting back on the many negative comments I'd endured from the lady at the foster home when I was younger.

"You're so ugly that even your toes are ugly! Yep! Ugly from head to toe," Leon would say while laughing, trying his best to pierce my spirit.

"You better look again," I'd fire back in an effort to shield my emotions to no avail. Nevertheless, I would often end up taking him back after the many break-ups. I feared being alone. Moreover, I kept this secret of abuse to myself, burying it inside me in order to avoid the embarrassment and shame of others knowing about it. I also wanted to protect my boyfriend from the wrath of my big brother, Bam. If he even suspected that I was being hurt or harmed by this man in any way, Leon would have to pay in blood. For some strange reason, I wanted to protect Leon in his brokenness. In doing so, his abuse not only continued, but got even worse.

A few days later I decided to go to the nail parlor to get some pampering, hoping to please him. I thought that maybe he would be pleased with my painted toenails. While walking toward the nail parlor I heard a man's voice: "Everything will be okay…try walking with your head up. You're beautiful," the man stated as I obliged, holding my head up and thanking him for his much-needed compliment. "Wow!" I thought to myself after looking at this man. He was absolutely stunning, looking as if he'd just walked off the cover of a magazine. On my way out of the nail parlor, another man was walking in. The handsome man looked down at my feet and said, "Your toes are beautiful. "Thank you," I replied as I headed out the door back home.

"Well, that was strange!" I thought to myself as I, unconsciously, continued to walk with my head down. In that moment I thought about Leon's negative comment and how the two men saw me so differently. The very words that came out of Leon's mouth in an effort to destroy my spirit, my Creator immediately intervened and said not so. I knew there was no truth in Leon's opinion of me. Though I felt somewhat empowered by the positive comments, the real issue at the time was

54

that I lacked self-love. So on this particular day, the two strangers reminded me of the self-love that I'd lost. I instantly held my head up after remembering the first man's suggestion. I also thought about how my daughter would be affected emotionally if I didn't find a way out of this situation. I loved her and knew it was my responsibility to protect her. At this time my daughter attended one of Ms. A's daycares. I was thankful that my daughter had the privilege of attending the daycare whenever I needed it. Plus, it protected her from seeing and hearing the abuse I was enduring.

On the way home I noticed I still had some time before picking my daughter up from the daycare. I then hurried in the house to the bathroom mirror in search of the beauty that the first man saw in me. It seemed like the confidence I used to have had vanished prior to my encounter with the two handsome men. "Who were they?" I thought as I stared at myself in the mirror, first gazing at my facial features before focusing in on my eyes. I wondered who or what was behind them as I examined my entire face. At that moment I thanked God for sending His two angels to remind me that I was created perfect in my Father's image, and that I was beautiful from head to toe.

Why was I afraid to use my voice to let someone know I was in an abusive relationship, you may ask? Because I was a secret keeper bounded by fear. I was protecting this person who said he loved me. I was also oblivious to what love really is. I had not yet healed from the ravages of my past trauma. I was too broken. Brokenness attracts brokenness! That's why I was so attracted to a broken boy addicted to alcohol, who behind closed doors had become a monster. I wanted to protect my child, and was also willing to protect Leon. Yet I failed to protect myself!

So I did the only thing I knew how to do. I prayed while standing there staring at the girl in the mirror as tears fell from her eyes. *"It's me again Father...I know that you are listening. Help me, Father...I need your help right now Lord. I want him away from me. He has hurt me. I am wounded..."* I went on praying, crying and pleading in the name of Jesus. As I ended my prayer I heard the front door open and footsteps getting closer. I turned on the faucet and splashed water on my face to wash away any evidence of the tears I had cried.

"Where's the car keys?" he demanded. "I'll be back," he said as soon as he had them in his hands. He didn't bother to mention when he planned to return. I walked over to the daycare, which was located directly across the street, to pick up my daughter. I remember being so happy to see my baby because her little face brought me so much joy in my pain. A few hours later Ms. A. called, wanting my daughter to spend the night with her because she'd gladly taken on the grandmother role. Her timing was perfect since I was contemplating how I was going to break out of the toxic relationship I was in. Well, there was at least one person who knew how unhappy I was. That person was Ivan, who was now serving a life sentence for an alleged murder.

Though I knew he was heavy into the street life, my mind couldn't process the crime he was accused and convicted of because he had never mistreated me. Sometimes I would secretly write to him, and even accept his phone calls during my many break-ups with Leon. Ivan's kind words brought me comfort while I was dealing with the abuse. That's just jail talk some of you may say. Well, Ivan never asked me for money. "Once I settle in, Ima send you money," Ivan stated. However, his one request was that I write to him. Therefore, it is my belief that God used Ivan in his time of trouble and brokenness, to bless me.

56

I say that because later on that night Leon came home drunk, demanding money. It was tax season and he knew I had money. "No, I need it. I have bills to pay," I explained. But before I knew it, he'd leaped on top of the bed with his shoes on and started punching me with all his might. I was dazed with the first blow. I couldn't believe the severity of the blows he was unleashing on me. The more I screamed, cried, and pleaded for him to stop, the more he delivered blows to my head. I grabbed a sheet from the bed and tried to shield my face, but it didn't help. I tried to kick him away as he stood over me, inflicting his pain upon me with not only his fists but his words.

"Bitch, you think I need you?? Well, I don't! I can't stand you!" he yelled while beating me.

"Stop! Stop! You're hurting me!" I screamed at the top of my lungs. "Take the money!" I pleaded with him. Then suddenly the phone rang, stopping Leon in his rage. I was undressed and disoriented and still trying to pull myself together as he answered the phone.

"It's a dude from jail...you talking to a dude in jail!?" he said while staring at me, laughing. He then accepted the call. I was terrified, not knowing if I should make a dash for the door or stand there frozen by the fear of being caught if I tripped in the process. I was afraid that if he caught me, the beating would be much worse. I decided to stand still. "He wanna speak to you. Come speak to him!" he demanded. "Come speak to him!" he yelled again. I hesitated to reach for the phone or even get near him. Proceeding with extreme caution, I walked over and took the phone.

"What's going on?" Ivan asked in an anxious yet concerned tone. "Are you okay? Is he putting his hands on you? He's not a man!" Ivan commented as he questioned Leon's manhood. I was no longer able to hold back my emotions. "I'm scared!" I screamed and cried on the phone. "I'm scared, okay?" I shouted, not wanting to mention the beating I'd just received.

"Put him on the phone!" Ivan demanded. "I need to speak to him now or do you want me to have somebody run up in your house and speak to him?" Confused by his question, I didn't know if he was telling me or asking me.

"No, don't do that!" I yelled, crying hysterically.

"Put him on the phone then!" Ivan demanded again.

I immediately handed Leon the phone, fearing that Ivan might carry out his threat to retaliate. I don't know what Ivan said to Leon, but the entire ordeal ceased immediately. There was complete silence. Leon didn't speak another word to me. Instead, he walked into the living room and sat down on the couch where he soon fell asleep. Meanwhile I went back into the bedroom to get dressed as I thought about my next move.

I could tell by his snoring that he was in a deep sleep. So I picked up the phone to call 911 just as morning approached. Moments later an officer arrived. I quickly told him about the ordeal I'd been through, and that I wanted my boyfriend out of my house. The officer entered the living room while Leon was still in a deep sleep. He first shined his flashlight on him, then called his name to wake him up. Leon woke up in a confused state and seemed startled by the presence of the policeman.

"What's going on officer?" he said, still drowsy. "I haven't done anything. Shay, tell him I've been right here sleeping." Leon immediately became defensive, hoping that I would back up his lie or that I'd protect him as I'd always done.

"Mr. Officer, this man has hurt me repeatedly, and I want him out now!" I assured the officer as tears fell from my eyes.

58

"Well sir…we've been called to this address before. Get up and get your things," the officer told Leon. "Get whatever you can now, and if you leave anything, an officer will or can be present while you get the remainder of your items." That day the relationship between Leon and I ended. I even filed a restraining order against him that I'd always failed to follow through with in the past. However, I did stop short of having him arrested. Nor did I press charges. In the end I guess I still protected him. Maybe God was protecting both of us that day in our brokenness. I also felt like God placed Ivan in my life for a reason, regardless of his transgressions.

Any one of us can be used by God, regardless of where we are on our life journey. I was a young girl who, at times, didn't make good decisions along the way. I didn't handle this situation in the proper manner, some may say. However, this is my testimony and I want to be truthful. In the end, I'm thankful that whenever I would call on my Father, He was there just as He said He would be, doing what He said He would do. I've forgiven Leon since then, but not before first forgiving myself for accepting and allowing someone to treat me in this manner. Forgiveness is not easy, but it had to be done in order for me to move on with my life. I also felt like there would be times when I would need forgiveness as well along the way as I searched for my purpose in life. So please, if you are in an abusive relationship, let someone know. Don't be a secret keeper like I was. Find the strength to let go and heal mentally, physically, and emotionally. Don't be ashamed or embarrassed, nor fear the judgment of others. Get help, say something, and protect yourself as well as your children, for God has created safe havens to protect His children. Therefore, don't be afraid or even hesitate to seek safe refuge or counsel!

Life kept moving along for me as I continued to try to find my purpose. I was a single mother now, and I was okay with that because I had managed to free myself from a toxic relationship. Not long after the ordeal with Leon, I received one last call from Ivan. "You don't really say much on the phone," he told me. "But you're cold with that pen." I didn't really think much about his comment at the time, but maybe he saw a talent in me that I just didn't see. But for some reason that comment always stuck close to my spirit.

I used to laugh at Ivan's efforts to try and rescue me in my youth, while I was still at the children's home. But I was thankful that God saw to it that he came to my rescue in perfect timing. Eventually, I stopped communicating with Ivan and moved on with my life. I guess I was too busy trying to figure out motherhood and adulthood, all while trying to grow into my own self-love. However, I have learned over the years to pay attention and to receive the messages and lessons from those who have entered my life. I am very thankful for all these individuals because they have played a part in shaping my character for something greater. It was the encounters, circumstances, and experiences in my life that ultimately helped me to recognize not only who I am, but whose I am.

Though life was far from perfect for me, I started noticing that I seemed to have favor and grace in my life while being confronted with very difficult circumstances. I didn't think much of it at the time, but later I learned that there is a process that the mind must go through before real change can occur, which is why I continued to be re-routed. One day, approximately six months after my twenty-third birthday, I went to work as usual. A few hours later Ms. A said, "Hey baby girl, I need to talk to you." Though I was 23 years old she still called me "baby girl." Maybe because I still had so much to learn and experience in this life.

I sat down in a chair as Ms. A began to talk. "Well baby girl, you know I love you," she told me. "And I will always be here for you... but you're 23 years old now, so today will be your last day working for me. It's time for you to go out and experience the real world on your own." As I sat there receiving Ms. A's tough love, my eyes immediately welled up with tears as I wondered what the real world was like. I quickly wiped away the tears before they fell from my face, but at the same time I noticed that Ms. A's eyes were also filled with tears as she turned around to gather her paperwork, not daring to let me see her cry. "I have to go now. I have a meeting to attend," she said as she walked quickly out the door.

Initially, I felt like she was pushing me away. But deep down I knew it was time for me to detach from Ms. A and the daycare center as well. After I'd had a good cry while sitting there wondering where I would find work to support my daughter and I, I received an instant message from my Father (God). He reminded me about the man at Evangelical Children's Home who had offered me employment back when I was 15 years old. I now heard the man's clear and concise voice in my ear just as if he had spoken to me yesterday: "Ms. Kennedy, you're gonna grow up and do great things. When you turn 21, come back and I'll employ you." I instantly wiped the tears from my face as I smiled, overjoyed by God's presence. It was His divine guidance that was now giving me directions on which route to take. At that moment I truly believed that my steps were being ordered by God.

Yes, I remembered saying I had no plans to return to the orphanage for any reason. At the time I wanted to put such places behind me for good. Which brings me back to that old saying: "If you ever want to make God laugh, tell Him your plans!" God's plan trumped my plan because He created me. Therefore, He knows my purpose and what's best for me. At the time, I didn't know what God was doing in my life, but He sure has a way of working things out.

The following Monday I headed to Evangelical Children's Home, trusting that Mr. Harris was still working there. I had not called to see if he was in his office on that particular day, however I expected him to be there. So I was ready for the interview and prepared to accept the job offer. I remember being a bit nervous because I was hoping he would still remember me and his kind offer. He did. Then he directed me to fill out the application. The position I applied for was as a residential worker, which required me to have experience working with children for at least two years. I easily met that qualification because of my work at the daycare for several years. Even though I didn't have a clue, God had already prepared me for the position.

A couple of weeks later I was interviewed and offered the position. I was so happy and thankful for this opportunity. Plus, I wanted Ms. A to be proud of me and see that I was able to "go out into the real world and make it on my own." I always wanted to be out on my own, but I also wanted to be just as successful as Ms. A. Instead, I was still under her umbrella because I was living in a house that she owned. A few months later, an opportunity presented itself. I ran into a daycare employee who informed me about a housing program called "Section 8" for low income individuals like myself.

Although I didn't know any details about this program, I was informed that my rent payments would be based on my income. I eventually attended the housing orientation and was given a voucher to reside in a property that would accept me. I already knew I wanted to choose a place close to the daycare because my daughter still went there. So I returned to the apartment complex where I had previously resided (when I was in the independent living program) to see if they would accept my voucher, and they did. Not long after, my daughter and I settled in.

Why was I being re-routed again, some of you may ask? Well I believe I was being re-routed by God so that He could show me a younger version of myself. At this time I still had no idea that God was using me. My first day on the job I would be working in the evenings with young girls who were placed in a locked unit because they were considered a high risk for running away. Each child, and the reason for their placement at the children's home, was different. So I didn't know what to expect on my first day. However, when I walked in, a child was enraged—throwing things, cursing, and screaming, "I wanna leave this f!?!ing place!"

Her outburst reminded me of the fits I used to have when I was younger and unable to see any future beyond the orphanage. There were so many occasions when I wanted to tell the girls: "I am you, and everything will be okay!" But instead, I buried my past experience of being an orphan with ease, and followed the policy of the children's home as instructed, which was never to discuss your personal life with the children. While being re-routed, my faith would be tested even more. Not to punish me, but to help me find and fulfill my true calling.

9

The Shift

MS. A'S QUESTION from years ago lingered in my mind. I was still unsure about what I wanted out of life. So I just went with the flow. Around this time I would see Buttercup occasionally. She still didn't like St. Louis County much but would still make time to come visit. She would also come with her book bag stuffed with notebooks, poems, and other writings. And just like before, she'd bring me a book that she thought I would enjoy. And as usual, I would put it away, showing no interest at the time.

It was like time was repeating itself. I was in the same place having the same experience with Buttercup. All we could think about was wanting a better life. We'd still laugh and giggle about the silliest things. Then I'd stare at her writings and say, "Keep up with all these writings because one day you will publish this, then we gonna be "in there like that that there." We would always use that slang expression, meaning we would no longer have to struggle financially because God would see to it that our misfortune worked out in our favor. I jumped up, breaking out in dance, laughing with excitement over the possibility. Then Buttercup and I would laugh some more. Though back then we had no clue about how to publish anything. Still, I believed in her so much that I believed it would happen one day. Then suddenly a shift occurred.

I saw Bam more frequently now. This particular day I received a call from him asking if I would mind him coming over to spend the weekend at my place. I didn't mind, and I was eager to spend some much-needed quality time with him because he was always moving around. Then he told me that someone would be dropping him off. I wondered where his car was but didn't question him about it. It wasn't unusual for him to not have transportation because he would often buy or sell his car, depending on his situation. Later on that night, he was dropped off and we talked and laughed as usual. But something was different. It seemed as if he was seeking to find peace and just wanted to rest awhile.

That Sunday things seemed fine. The music was turned up a bit as I sang along while driving him to a friend's house. I turned to him expecting a funny remark or laughter because of my singing, but instead I saw a tear fall from his eye. I nervously reached over to turn down the radio. "Bam, what's wrong?" I asked anxiously. "Is everything okay?" Instantly I was scared and worried. I hadn't seen my big brother shed tears since we were children.

I didn't give him a chance to answer before firing more questions. "Is someone after you? Did you do anything?" I questioned him non-stop as tears formed in my eyes. Bam never wanted us to worry about him. He always kept his issues hidden from my sisters and me. But I continued pressing him for an answer. Finally, he looked at me and said, "It's this life; I'm just tired." It seemed to me that his pain and frustration was ready to burst out of his body in order to free his soul. My heart felt so heavy, but there was nothing I could do at that moment to fix the situation or to help him. I drove down the highway silent, in tears, saddened as my brother sat there exhausted from all that he had been through and endured. And yet he seemed to be carrying our pain as well.

I pulled up to his destination, glancing around for potential danger, worried about his safety. Before getting out of the car, my brother hugged me and kissed me on the cheek. "I love you…I'll call you later," was all he said as he got out of the car. "Okay," I replied as I drove off slowly, gazing in the rear view mirror to see which house or what direction he was headed in. He walked straight, with his head down, not giving me a clue as to where he was going. I wondered if things would be okay as I turned the corner, feeling sad. Later on that night I called to check on him, and he assured me that he was okay. I felt somewhat relieved after speaking with him. I thought that maybe he was just having a moment like we all have at times when the load gets a little too heavy.

I went to work as usual that day, putting on a fake smile in an effort to mask the pain of what my brother was experiencing. Plus, I wanted to appear strong for the girls in the home since I saw myself through them. A week later, while at work, I received a call from Buttercup that was heartbreaking. She told me that Bam had been murdered. I was numb and confused as I left work crying, wondering why God had taken our big brother from us.

To be honest, I didn't want to accept the news that I'd heard from Buttercup. So I called Linda, who was a mother figure to Bam, in the hope that I would hear something different. Linda confirmed that my big brother had indeed been gunned down. She also asked my sisters and me to meet her at the coroner's office so that his next of kin could identify the body. I was devastated. My heart was broken into little pieces. Though I knew I was never supposed to question God, I did that day.

"God, why have you allowed our big brother to be taken from

us?" I screamed. I was furious with God that day as I continued to cry while questioning him. "My brother was all we had to watch over us and protect us!" I cried uncontrollably. "Who do we have now, God?" I screamed.

Finally, I arrived at the coroner's office where I would meet Linda, Buttercup, and Shaunta. We had to decide who would identify my brother's body. Since Buttercup was the oldest, it was decided that she would be the one who would view Bam's lifeless body. Although the rest of us didn't think she could handle seeing him in this state, she insisted. Buttercup and Bam were very close, and I personally didn't believe that Buttercup would be able to cope after witnessing such a sight. Especially given how she'd been affected by the trauma of my mother's death. After my brother's funeral, I knew I had to be even stronger for Buttercup, for my daughter, my other siblings, as well as the girls I worked with at the children's home. Though my world had been ripped apart by traumatic challenges, I absolutely refused to let life knock me down.

During this time I became aware of a hidden blessing in my life. I discovered that working at the children's home was equipping me with skills that I was able to apply to my everyday life. The children's home scheduled mandatory class meetings which provided me with the opportunity to learn even more about children. I learned about the girls' various backgrounds, the environments they were raised in, as well as their changes in mental states and behaviors following traumatic events in their lives.

In addition to this knowledge, the experience I was receiving by working with the girls gave me insight into many of their behaviors and emotional triggers. I also gained knowledge about different types of behavior disorders which a few of the girls at the home suffered from. These classes gave me a better understanding of family structures and dynamics, as well as substance abuse, rape, domestic violence, and self-harm among other issues. Day by day I was learning just how broken my own family was. Working with the girls and learning more about family dynamics gave me greater confidence as I began to apply this knowledge in my everyday life. Working at the children's home gave me strength to endure as I searched for my life's purpose, even though I still had no voice. Believe it or not, I was still ashamed and embarrassed about my experience of being an orphan.

Meanwhile I hadn't heard from Buttercup in a few months. She stopped calling and no longer came to the county to see me. I had a lot of sleepless nights wondering about where she was and how she was doing. I knew my brother's death was taking a heavy toll on her. Buttercup seemed to be losing her mind after Bam's death. After weeks of worrying, Buttercup finally called me, but she didn't seem like herself. She was no longer rational. I got scared when her conversation with me became bizarre. The laughter that once connected us was gone. Immediately, I sensed in her voice that something was very wrong about her.

"Are you okay, Buttercup?" I asked anxiously.

"You have your own street with your name on it," she said.

"Buttercup are you okay?" I yelled, starting to get upset. "Something is wrong, Buttercup," I told her. "Where are you?"

"Girl, goodbye! You don't have to believe me," she said, becoming upset. Then she hung up the phone. I became concerned about her mental state, especially as I learned more about mental health, its symptoms and triggers. I was scared for Buttercup. But I was frightened even more about the possibility of losing the indispensable bond we shared as sisters. I needed her to stay strong for me as I tried to stay strong for her!

Sometime later I received a call from a friend asking if I knew whether or not Buttercup was on drugs. "I don't believe so," I responded. But I didn't really know. Days later, another person informed me that they saw Buttercup in a well-known drug area. I didn't want to discuss my sister's possible mental health issues even with friends. Nor did I want to believe that she was using drugs. But shortly afterwards I found out that crack cocaine had indeed manifested itself in her life as well.

Buttercup's mental health went undiagnosed and untreated for quite a while. Sometimes I would speak to her, and it would seem as if she was back to her old self again. At other times, her thoughts and conversation seemed weird and bizarre. One day when I spoke to her she expressed her thoughts very clearly. I was shocked and downhearted after Buttercup told me that she decided to use crack cocaine in order to experience what Mama had felt. I burst into tears as I listened to her because I wanted her to be strong with me. I didn't want to be strong alone. Yet, at that moment, I knew that I would have to be strong for all of us.

I remembered back to when we were younger and Grandma Rose would make us clean out the closet. I would leave Buttercup to do all the work as I sat doing nothing but cracking jokes to make her laugh. I always loved laughter. When Buttercup got tired of doing the chores alone (and of my silliness), she'd scream: "Grandmamaaaaa! Bootie ain't helping...she's sitting down."

"No I'm not Grandma," I'd chime in while making a mean face at Buttercup.

"With your lazy self!" Buttercup would fire back.

Then we would go back and forth with one another until Grandma came and spanked both of us for fussing. After making sure the coast was clear, I'd tease Buttercup, happy about the fact that she got a spanking, too.

"That's what you get for being a tattletale," I'd say to her.

"Well, at least I'm not a crybaby like you!"

"So! I'm still not doing anything...and how did she fit all this stuff in this little bitty closet anyway?" I asked Buttercup while making a funny face. Then we'd both bust out laughing, puzzled because neither of us could figure out how Grandma managed to put so much stuff in such a small closet. In the end, Buttercup would still end up doing the chores alone as I entertained her with more of my silliness.

After reflecting back on all those days that she had carried the weight alone on behalf of all of us, I decided that it was my turn to be strong for Buttercup. I really wanted to prove to Buttercup that I wasn't lazy. I decided that I would be strong for all of us now.

So, as you can see, I could never get away from my nickname— Bootie—no matter how hard I tried. We three older siblings all had very provocative nicknames: Bam, Buttercup, and Bootie. Our nicknames make us sound like exotic characters out of a book. How awesome! Because you're reading that book right now! For a long time I didn't want anyone to know my nickname was Bootie. Now I'm so glad that God took the shame away, making it possible for me to give true testimony as I return to my real life drama.

During another one of our calls, Buttercup said: "I'm just tired sis... I can't seem to cope with this life. You are stronger than I am!"

"I'm not stronger, I just can't give up! Can't you see that I'm hurting, too?" I fussed at her as I wept. I tried so hard to understand her reasoning for making the decision to use the very drug that had destroyed our family. I'd lie in bed at night still wondering what would become of my siblings and me. The shift that was occurring in my life caused me to wonder if my family had been cursed. I'd lost Mama, Bam, Grandma Rose, Grandpa Eddie, and now seemingly Buttercup. I didn't understand why things were continuously unfolding the way they were.

I was about 24 years old around this time. And yes, I was still a secret keeper. Even at this point I wouldn't speak about my childhood nor how things were turning out for my siblings and me in our adulthood. Still ashamed and embarrassed about my family's misfortune, I dared not share any part of my life with anyone. I hid the pain inside as I "glammed up" my body on the outside. And besides, if I ran into anyone who remembered me from an orphanage or foster home, they would see from my trendy outside appearance that I was doing just fine. And should anyone ask how I was doing, they would be met with the same answer: "I'm doing just fine." I didn't want anyone's sympathy because I figured that nobody but God could fix the shame, pain, and hurt that I was enduring.

However, there were times when I would stop speaking to God for a little while as I tried to fix my life on my own. How many of you out there know that without God, we can do nothing? But God also gives His children free will, and I was happy about that because it meant I was

71

allowed to do things my way. Though it took some time, I regained my confidence after Bam's death just as I did following the abuse by Leon.

I was young, bold, beautiful, and assertive. And to be completely honest, sometimes I did like many of you have done when you feel desperate and cornered. Yes, I said, "Fuck it!" And I stopped caring for just a little while. I partied and kicked it hard. I hardened my heart as I dressed up my pain, glamorized it, and made it look good while I was doing it—or so I thought. Whenever I was off work I wanted to go out. I drank, smoke, entertained unhealthy relationships, had sex, made poor decisions regarding the men I chose, made poor decisions with the money I was blessed with, had abortions—and my tongue became a lethal weapon.

And yes, during all of these lonely and desperate activities, what I lacked most of all was self-love. But I had to travel that path in order to grow, as well as to help someone else. By sharing my truth, I hope that some young girl out there somewhere will make better choices than I did. I made so many poor choices during that time. Still, if I could go back and speak to the younger me, I'd forgive her. Remember, it's never too late to forgive yourself. And you do this by first taking ownership for your actions. Let God be the judge. And let he who is without sin cast the first stone!

However, since I am God's child, I also begged for my Father's forgiveness. I always knew that God had a plan for my life. Buried in my heart there was always this feeling of knowing that I was to do something, accomplish something more, or complete a special task. The partying didn't last for long, and I soon realized that there was no escaping the life that I was given, nor deviating from the purpose for which I was created. Without a doubt this purpose was to serve. These words came to me out of my spirit: "Accept both the mother and the life that I have chosen for you. Now go and know that I am God."

By trying to get off my appointed path, by attempting to sabotage my life purpose while deliberately choosing to live life unconsciously, I was regressing instead of progressing. It was complete nonsense to think that I could fix my life on my own. In my attempt, I bumped and banged my head along the way. I was only wounding myself, causing myself even more pain. Once again, I felt defeated. Know that whenever you seem to get off track—or whenever there is a shift in your life—know that God is still with you. He is still guiding, leading, and directing you towards what is destined for your life. I knew I was making poor decisions, so I stopped for a moment and got still to ask God to forgive me for my wrongdoings. However, my faith was about to be tested even more. I would need even more strength to endure the devastating impact of the life challenges that were headed toward me. So I braced myself for the blow.

Although the phase in my life described above was difficult, I pulled myself together and resolved to make better decisions as I tried to be strong alone. But how many of you out there know that I wasn't alone? Know that God will never leave you nor forsake you! Understand that life will unfold for you the way it chooses, without your permission and without warning.

This particular day I was off work when I received a call from Ms. A saying she wanted me to take a ride with her because she needed to speak with me about something important. I figured it was good news, maybe news about a new business venture that she wanted to share with me. She'd always get excited when things worked out, and I would be just as excited for her. I also knew that this "talk" wasn't about me because I was working, being a good mother, and now doing my best to make better choices. Plus, I was no longer under her umbrella.

I was excited to see her because so much had transpired in my life. I didn't see her as often now that I was seriously taking on both adulthood and motherhood. Her timing was perfect, I thought, because she always offered me such good advice. I also thought we might catch up on the latest events unfolding in our lives. Ms. A was humorous too, and I was always up for a good laugh. I couldn't wait to spend some much-needed time with her. Finally she arrived. When I got in the car I could sense that something was wrong. Instantly, I became concerned judging by her demeanor and body language. Maybe this wasn't good news, I thought. I searched her face for emotions that might give me a clue about what was going on. But her expression was neither happy nor sad.

"Ms. A....is everything okay?" I asked.

"Baby girl, I'm gonna tell you something, and I need you to be strong for me," she said while driving. I immediately thought about my daughter, my siblings, and the girls at the children's home whom I had already decided to be strong for. So there was no doubt in my mind that I could be strong for Ms. A as well. "Okay," I replied as I waited nervously for her to speak. Though nothing could have prepared me for the news she was about to deliver.

"I'm dying baby girl," she said.

"You dying??" I asked in disbelief. My stomach dropped as I squeezed the seat with my sweaty palms. I was confused because she looked amazing and perfectly healthy. I was numb as the car pulled up to a medical building. Ms. A's news had silenced me as I thought of losing her.

"I'll be right back. I have to pick up some paperwork," she said abruptly as she stepped out of the car, letting the door slam behind her. Right then I spoke to my divine Father: *"Oh God, please save her. I don't understand what's happening,"* I prayed while Ms. A was still inside the medical building. But moments later she showed back up carrying a large yellow envelope.

"I'm a fighter," she said without conviction.

"Everything will be okay," I said to her as I tried to reassure both her and myself at the same time. We then had lunch and went over her treatment options and plans.

I suddenly changed my mind about sharing any news in my life with her, and especially about Buttercup. She already had enough on her plate. Life was again unfolding for me without warning or permission. I didn't understand what God was doing in my life and I soon fell into depression. It became a struggle for me to get out of bed to care for my daughter, and to go to work as well. I soon found myself lying in bed asking God to not only restore Buttercup's mind, but to keep my mind as well. Too much was happening too soon, so I kept on praying. I hadn't heard from Buttercup in a while. I worried about her safety and well-being. I often prayed that God would watch over her and protect her. After I would pray for her, she'd call. Prayer works.

This particular day, Buttercup seemed fine but disappointed because she had lost the book bag that contained all of her writings. Happy just to talk to her, I immediately tried to connect with her through laughter. "We was gonna be in there like that, that there," I said to her, although

I was just as disappointed as she was about her losing the book bag. I believed that one day she would publish her writings in the hope that we would live a life beyond our wildest imagination.

You see, it was my belief, but it was Buttercup's work. At that time I didn't have the courage to do my own work. Or as Buttercup would say back when we were younger: "Bootie being lazy."

"So you mean to tell me that you have no idea where you lost the book bag?" I asked Buttercup in disbelief. "Tell me you got chased by a dog," I said, making light of the situation because Buttercup was afraid of dogs. We both burst into laughter, finding humor in our pain. I informed her about the devastating news regarding Ms. A.

"Everything is going to be okay sis," she said.

"I love you, Buttercup," I said to her before ending our call.

Some months later, Ms. A would be placed on hospice. She had become very frail due to the cancer that was taking over her body, but she was still able to speak. I sat at her bedside heartbroken as she struggled to speak those painful words once more: "I'm dying, baby girl. I can't fight anymore...I'm tired now." I wept as I expressed my gratitude for her being in my life.

"I love and thank you, Ms. A," I told her, "for not only accepting me, but loving me as your own. I thank you for leading by example, for equipping me with the necessary tools and knowledge to flourish, then pushing me out into "the real world.""

"Thank you so much for making me repeat that slogan—I can, I will, and I am!—in the hope that one day I might believe in myself. You fought a good fight...teaching me to never give up! So I thank you for showing me the true essence of a woman. And most importantly, for showing me a mother's love."

76

The following day Ms. A passed on. I broke down as I stood in the corner watching as the coroner zipped up the body bag, then wheeled her lifeless body away on a gurney. That day I cried uncontrollably, not only for Ms. A, but as I remembered Mama's death as well.

After my life shifted, I decided to work only as needed at the children's home so I could focus on taking care of myself. I felt alone, angry, and frustrated as I continued to try to find my purpose in life. Shortly afterwards, I was let go from my job at the children's home for failing to work enough hours. I was 25 years old now, but even after Ms. A's death I could still hear her voice: "Baby girl, what do you want out of life?"

I knew I wanted to be successful, just as she had been. But I didn't have a clue as to how I would achieve my desire. Although Ms. A's college degree had nothing to do with her success, I did just as she suggested. I enrolled at the local college. Not long after, I seemed to be running into more financial obligations due to previous debts. I decided to drop out of school to work. I was impatient, often thinking about how long it would take to receive a degree in order to become successful.

I felt like I needed a degree in order to be successful. But once again, God's plans for one's purpose will often differ. This is my story, however, you will absolutely need to be educated as you pursue certain fields that you may be interested in (i.e. lawyer, doctor, judge). But a degree does not guarantee one's success. And as Ms. Oprah Winfrey has said: "A degree may be utilized best when it is used so that you may be of service to others." Your service to others, if rendered with love and sincerity, will then bring about success according to your heart's intention.

In addition, for those of you who don't have a degree, or you have decided that college is not for you, you must be creative. It is your responsibility to find your purpose, which may also be found through your God given gifts or talents. However, in order to live the life you want, you MUST learn to be of service to others. It doesn't matter whether you feel your calling is to get involved with or start a business, or create a product or service; each of these can benefit someone else. But whatever you choose, you must act on it. It may require you to study, research, practice or become educated in a specific area. However, don't give up. Complete the task by doing whatever it takes to accomplish your dreams! Give of yourself. Learn to be of service to others. You must sow a seed to prosper, having good intentions within your heart as you do so.

I went on with my life after deciding to drop out of school. I had no clue which path I was to take nor where I would find employment. I also still chose to conform to tradition by working a nine-to-five job. There's absolutely nothing wrong with working a job if that's what you want and choose to do. Though I was a good worker, I struggled with routine, with doing the same thing at the same time day after day. And while growing up, there was always this feeling of knowing that there was something more for me. I knew I was supposed to accomplish a particular thing, although I didn't know what it was. And until I found out what the "more" or the "it" was, I was willing to keep searching.

During my quest, I was often left feeling unfulfilled, unhappy, and I continued to be surrounded by debt. After all that had transpired, I soon realized that I alone could not carry this weight on my own. I was not able to be strong for anyone before I could first be strong for myself. And so I prayed, placing my burdens upon the Lord. I cried out to my

Father saying, *"Father God, help me! I feel so alone! I need you right now, Lord! I ask that you give me strength...I can't do anything without you, Father. I place my burdens upon you, God. Please lead me, guide me, and give me direction Father, because I am lost without you. Lord, I ask that you show me the way. I ask that you order my footsteps...in Jesus' name I pray. Amen."*

After I prayed, I decided to straighten up the house a bit. I noticed that I'd cleaned everything in the apartment except the closet. I was reluctant to clean it out because I'd managed to put so much stuff in this small closet. I smirked as I reminisced about how Grandma Rose would do the same thing. I then proceeded to start at the top of the closet where I'd been storing and collecting the books that Buttercup had given me. I smiled as I picked up one of the books. I could hear her voice when she would say, "Girl, read the book. You're gonna love it!" I then opened the book to the first chapter to see if it would capture my attention.

It did, and I couldn't stop reading. I was completely captivated. It seemed as if I had become the character in the book, or at least I imagined myself to be. I didn't finish cleaning the closet that day. Instead, I found myself immersed in this book. Then afterwards, I continued to read book after book after book. I'd come a long way on my journey only to find out that my journey had just begun.

10
Order My Footsteps

A FEW DAYS later a friend of mine called to see how I was doing. He also told me that he was about to go to the library to check out a few books. Remember, there's no such thing as a coincidence, and nothing just happens. Therefore, I couldn't pass up the opportunity to join him. When we arrived he suggested a few books that would make me feel better, as well as books that would also shift my thinking. After scanning through the books that he suggested, I decided to check them out.

But not before noticing that I was standing in the "Self-Help" aisle. I was surprised that there were so many books to choose from. I needed all the help I could get, and decided to check out as many books as allowed. Growing up, there was a definite stigma attached to seeing a therapist. When I was a little girl, I can remember being told "what goes on in this house, stays in this house." So I went years without seeking professional help or getting a clear understanding of my thoughts and emotions. Now I was thankful for books, because for me they came to represent an alternate path to the healing power I needed most during this time. After reading so many books, one day I received an instant message from my Father. This message came to me in the form of a clear thought, in hopes that I would find my purpose.

There are some thoughts—very special ones—that are a pure gift to us from our Creator. After receiving this blessed thought I was prompted to write my own book and share my story with the world. However, the shame I felt because of the many challenges I'd had to face in my life rendered me powerless. Though I'd read books on positive thinking as well as other self-help books, I allowed fear to creep in. I lacked self-belief. For this reason I was not obedient to the call placed on my life as I told myself a story with shame and guilt attached to it.

Therefore, it was shame and guilt together that said to me: "Nobody wants to read a book written by an uneducated orphan." I felt like I was unqualified to do what I was called to do. Oblivious to the fact that God had already deemed me qualified. Where was my faith after God had answered my prayers time after time, you may ask? Truth is, I unconsciously managed to bury my faith underneath the pain I'd held on to. After writing only a few sentences of the book, I put my dream away in the closet and chose to let it die.

Though I felt like a failure for not going after my dream, I thoroughly enjoyed my newfound passion for books. But in spite of my concerns about finding and acting on my purpose, life continued to move forward. Once again I found myself desperately seeking employment to provide for my daughter and myself. I began submitting more applications, though I really wanted to take a break from working with children and focus on my own life.

But God chose to intervene once again and placed me right back on the path towards my destiny. Nevertheless, I was still unaware of God's plan as I applied mostly for factory or warehouse type jobs. Meanwhile the bills were piling up as I waited to be hired at one of these factories. Maybe I hadn't received any calls because of my lack of experience in doing this type of work, I thought. Frustrated, I thought surely I can gain employment in the one field where I possess both knowledge and experience! So I decided to seek employment at Marygrove Children's Home. Or was it God's will? Because I was being sent back to the very place I'd been ashamed of when I was approved for the independent living apartment. I could remember being elated that the apartment was not located on the campus. And still I was blind to the blessing!

Looking back, I believe that my footsteps were being ordered back to the place where guilt and shame gained the upper hand in my life. The error of my ways was being manifested a second time. Again, God was showing me my younger self as an orphan in the hope that I would gain the courage to confront and salve my own wounds. Only through healing would I be able to fulfill my life's purpose. My Father never left me as He continued to place me on the path towards my destiny.

Once I went through the application process, I was interviewed and hired immediately. I was overjoyed and abundantly grateful to my Father (God) for His grace and favor. I accepted the position as a residential worker, which meant I would be working with young girls from ages 5-12 years of age. I enjoyed working with the girls. I assisted them with their daily living skills, encouraged them to make good choices, and let them know that it was possible for them to achieve their goals and dreams if they dared not to give up. Working with the girls also helped me to heal by causing me to look past my own pain.

Whenever I was at work, I would be present in the moment, forgetting about my own issues in order to meet someone else's needs. Again I wanted to tell the girls: "I am you, and everything will be okay." However, I buried my past experience of being an orphan with ease as I followed the institution's policy, which was to never discuss your personal issues with the children. Though I was being of service, I felt like I was doing a disservice to myself as well as to the very children I said I would be strong for by being voiceless. My time here had come to an end because I was still ashamed and not yet ready to do what God had called me to do.

After about six months, I was let go from this position for failure to obtain a valid driver's license. You see, I had previous traffic tickets that I'd failed to pay in a timely manner, which eventually resulted in my driver's license being revoked. In my position as a residential worker, a valid driver's license was essential to take the children on planned outings, or to pick them up or drop them off at school or for other activities. Without a job, my household debts began to mount up just like before. Remember nothing just happens. I believe that being let go from this position was part of God's plan because I had more life lessons to learn before I would let go of the shame and gain the courage to share my story with the world. It was time for me to move on in my journey as I searched not only for who I was, but the purpose for which I was created. Truth is, it was time for me to be obedient to the call of action that God had placed on my life.

11

Changing My Thoughts

ALMOST TEN YEARS went by. Meanwhile I spent most of that time doing a little bit of this and a little bit of that, and still being unsure about what I wanted to do or become. No matter where I ended up, I'd tell myself, "There's something more that I need to accomplish."

I put the orphanage and my pain-filled past behind me. I worked several different jobs that didn't pay much after working at the children's home. I was struggling to make ends meet. I was still in the Section 8 program, and was receiving food stamps as well as Medicaid. I remember saying to myself: "One day I will no longer be a part of this housing program; I will be able to pay my own rent. God, I want to make two or three times more than what I'm making now."

The words I spoke eventually came to pass when I landed a job at the United States Postal Service. I thought I'd finally made it because I'd landed "a good job." Although I was thankful for the new opportunity and the fact that I was making more money, I was still not happy or fulfilled. I was managing the best I could as a single mother of two now. I juggled paying off previous debts, my current bills, as well as providing for my children.

While working at the post office, I would often tell myself (or rather, the spirit within me): "This is not it. There's something more for me to accomplish. I want joy, fulfillment, and abundance." I noticed that my postal job was across the street from Echo Children's Home where I once lived. I just couldn't seem to get away from my past! So I figured I might as well trust the process as I struggled to conform to my daily routine of going to work while basically doing the same things. Still I could hear Ms. A's words that had pierced my spirit: "Baby girl, what do you want out of life?" And still, after all this time, I could not answer such a simple question.

Not long after, I spoke to a friend of mine who once helped me through a dark time in my life by suggesting certain self-help books. Well, after many sleepless nights of complaining about my bills and frustration over life's adversities, this same person suggested that I had to change my thoughts in order to change my life. Thankful for his suggestion, I did just that: I changed my thoughts in order to change my life. I read certain scriptures over and over as well as more books that would help me change my mindset. I listened to audio tapes until positive thoughts were embedded and received in my subconscious mind.

I then realized that I was still holding on to the nickname "Shay" that I'd created while at the children's home. I'd used this nickname as a defense mechanism at the time due to the environment. I now wanted to rid myself of the often negative ego that came with using this nickname. Some people still refer to me as Shay, but I know who I am. I even questioned my birth name, Daphine, which was given to me. I wondered who I was without the name. Immediately, I cried out to my Father (God) and asked, "Who am I? Who am I?" A subtle voice replied: "I am your Father, The Creator of all that is, and you are my child."

Immediately, I noticed a feeling of peace. Complete peace. "I am God's child!" I said courageously with conviction. I was now clear about whose I was as well as who I am. Despite my family's misfortune, I declared that with the help of I Am (God) I would turn things around. I am God's child, a spirit being having a human experience. Though I experienced being an orphan, I now know that being an orphan does not define me. My experiences were all a part of God's plan. God created me, loves me, and knows what's best for me. Therefore, God has had to shape and mold me so that His light may shine through me. Though many of the devastating experiences of my life were difficult to experience, they were only blessings in disguise. They were placed along my path to help build my character and to prepare me for something greater. I had to endure them in order to give true testimony.

God continued to answer my prayers, and Buttercup eventually received the proper treatment for her mental health issues, which restored her mind. I was thankful because her thoughts were now rational, though she still struggled with her addiction. I continued to pray for her rehabilitation. Please remember that "faith without works is dead." I was grateful that I was able to reconnect with Buttercup through laughter again, but what I wanted most was for her to be whole, healed completely.

As for Shaunta, she is now a single mother of two. Her son is the first person in our family to attend a four year university. My two younger siblings (who were officially adopted) searched for us, and we were all reunited. On a few occasions, we were all able to be in the same room at the same time. As we thoroughly enjoyed one another, once again it was laughter that connected us, helping us to forget all that we had endured.

However, it was obvious that even as adults the poverty mindset was still present. At times it would become depressing to sit around and watch my siblings struggling; some of us were still not able to enjoy special family moments because of lack of money. At times, I would even distance myself from my siblings to avoid watching them struggle without a way to help. Though I had a "good job" at the United States Postal Service, I struggled financially as well. So I changed my thoughts in order to help change our lives.

I did the only thing I could do. I prayed. But this time my prayer was different.

"Father I am your child, and I love you with all my might, my heart, and my soul. I thank You for all of Your many blessings. Thank you for protecting me and watching over my family, as it was You who rewarded us and allowed us another day to live on this earth that you have created. Father, you get all the praise and glory. I also thank you for all the individuals that you have allowed to enter my life. Thank you for the good times and the difficult moments. It was Your will for my life, Father, even though I was blind to your blessings as You walked with me, never leaving me nor forsaking me as you brought me through the hardships that shaped and molded me. Please forgive me Father for my many wrongdoings. And thank you Father for allowing me to feel defeated as I tried to control Your plan for my life at times. Father God, I ask that You let Your will for my life be done. Father, I surrender Lord. I ask that You use me right now, Father. Use me, Father! I want to be a blessing to others! Use me so that I'm able to inspire millions of people. I want joy, fulfillment, and abundance. I want to be able to provide for not only myself but my family as well. Father God, I can't do anything without you. Show me the way. Show me Your way, Lord! Use me, Father, in Jesus' name!" I said as I cried and ended my prayer.

After I'd finished praying, I suddenly realized I'd forgot to ask God what my purpose was here on this earth. So I spoke to my Father once again, saying: *"Father…it's me again, your daughter. What is my purpose here on this earth?"* A subtle voice replied: **"I send you upon the earth in hopes that you yourself will find your purpose. I have blessed all of my children with certain gifts and talents. Remember, you are a spirit being in body form, powerful. Therefore, you must learn to operate from that being which is spirit. Trust me, daughter. Everything is orchestrated by me, The Creator. You are my child… therefore, you too have the ability to create. Now go and know that I am God."**

12

Believe

MY DAUGHTER D'Chyra is now 17 years old. I also have a young son, Brandon. I tell my daughter daily to go after her dreams. I often say to my daughter, "Do your very best while you're in school. Find your purpose, and never give up on your dreams." But one day I overheard myself making this statement with frustration in my voice: "Don't forget to go after your dreams!" I said to her. At that moment I realized that I was actually speaking to myself. Or was it my spirit speaking to me?

A few days later, which was on a Sunday, my daughter asked if I would join her for a jog. After jogging she asked, "Mama, what do you want to do next?" I replied, "Let's go to the library." She agreed with a smile because she knew how much I loved books and enjoyed the atmosphere of the library. So we headed to our local library only to find out that it was closed because it was Sunday. "Let's go to Barnes & Noble," I said. When we walked into the bookstore, there was a display of new books right in front of us. One particular book caught my attention because the man pictured on its cover was dressed for success.

I immediately thought of Ms. A's success, and how well-dressed she would be for meetings or just simply to run errands. I wanted to be just as successful as Ms. A had been, or even more! I smiled as I pictured myself being dressed for success. And still I had no clue of how I would achieve my desires at the time. I walked right past the book with the well-dressed man on the cover. This book seemed to have some sort of energy coming from it. But I ignored my impulse to check out the book and who the man was on the cover. I just kept walking and browsing for more books that would strengthen my belief in myself. Plus, for some reason I thought that maybe I might run into someone who knew about publishing.

The thought also crossed my mind that I should go back to writing the book that I'd started ten years ago. It was just a thought. But thoughts turn into things, I reminded myself. Constantly, I wondered how the book would be manifest. I knew absolutely nothing about publishing. Then, as I was walking down the aisle, I noticed a very tall man with a big curly afro who was strangely dressed in black and white checkered pants and red shoes. Maybe he's a musician, I thought to myself as I watched him pick up a book about Prince. I nudged my daughter, trying to get her to look at the man's attire. Yes, I still love laughter and being a little silly at times!

The man looked very interesting, and I tried not to chuckle. Instead, I smiled and asked the man if he knew anything about publishing.

"Yes, you want to get yourself a good publicist," the strangely dressed man said.

"No...publishing sir. Do you know anything about publishing?" I asked again.

"Make sure you get yourself a good publicist," the man stated again.

"Okay, thank you sir," I replied as I moved on. I didn't know what God was doing, but my Father sure does have a sense of humor, I thought as I smiled. I knew I was in this bookstore at this particular time for a reason. "Nothing just happens. Everything is orchestrated by me, Your Father," my spirit spoke to me as I moved along the bookstore aisles. I proceeded to walk to the other side of the store where I noticed a woman looking at journals. I asked the lady if she knew anything about publishing, expressing my desire to inspire children who were living in orphanages and in foster homes.

"Don't worry about the how, your book will be published," the lady said. "Devon was here last night," the lady proceeded to say as if I knew who she was speaking about.

"Who?" I asked with a clueless look on my face.

"DeVon…DeVon Franklin," she said, repeating his name.

"I'm sorry, but I don't know him," I told her.

"His book is located on the display right as you walk in," she informed me. She was speaking of the man on the book cover I'd noticed when I walked in the bookstore.

"Look him up…and check out his sermons when you get a chance."

"Okay," I replied. Well that was strange, I thought to myself. I'd been re-routed back to the book with the well-dressed man on the cover. I didn't purchase anything. Instead, I received three messages that day. First, the strangely dressed man stating, "Get yourself a good publicist!" Then the advice offered by the lady: "Don't worry about the how, because your book will be published." And last, I was to "look up DeVon Franklin."

"Thank you Jesus," I whispered as I smiled, knowing that my Father was present. There was this feeling of knowing that God was leading, guiding, and showing me the way. God was conspiring with me to help me to write my book! I couldn't wait to make it home so I could look up DeVon Franklin. I told my daughter I was going to go after my dream and finish the book that I'd started ten years ago.

"You can do it, Mama," my daughter said. When I got home I went to my room, closed the door, and began writing. I didn't have a computer, so I decided to use my cell phone. Moments later, my daughter came in with a notebook. It was the original notebook from ten years ago that I'd buried in the closet of the house where we were now living. Wow! That was perfect timing—or was it God's timing because many of the original notes I'd written were right there in the notebook. It was a difficult and emotional moment for me as I got right into it, typing the story directly into my phone without even bothering to write an introduction.

After getting through the second chapter, I decided to take a break because it seemed as if I was reliving the story, which brought up many strong emotions. Since I was taking a break from writing at that moment, I decided to look up the guy on the book cover—DeVon Franklin. I quickly discovered that he had been given a gift to minister, and that he was also the best-selling author of The Hollywood Commandments, among other achievements. On the first video I chose to watch, DeVon was saying: "It's somebody out there who put away a dream almost ten years ago!" Instantly, I believed!

"That's me!" I shouted aloud with conviction as if someone was in the room with me. I'd finally found my purpose. How did I know that I'd found my purpose, some of you may ask? Well, because I no longer felt the need to deny or resist my experience of being an orphan. I no longer felt ashamed. I knew now that it was all on purpose! I also knew that my purpose here on this earth is to serve. I recalled my heartfelt prayer: "Use me, Father!" My prayer was now being answered since I was no longer resisting. Instead, I was accepting and embracing my experience of being an orphan by sharing my story with the world without shame.

Well, I'd obviously never written a book before. But I'd heard and read that if you wanted to be successful, that it was in your best interest to have a mentor. But I didn't have a mentor. So I decided to look up St. Louis writers. I thought that I would reach out to someone in my city who was an experienced writer for advice on book writing. I proceeded to type in St. Louis writers on Google, and the late great Ms. Maya Angelou popped up. Though Ms. Maya Angelou has since passed on, I immediately showed her love and gratitude by saying, "Thank you, Ms. Maya Angelou for paving the way for me. It is because of your example and service that I know that I can write this book and accomplish my dream."

After thanking Ms. Maya Angelou, I thought of a quote that I'd posted online as my profile picture that read: "You lack nothing. Use what I gave you! - God." Okay, Father, I said to myself (to my inner spirit), I accept the challenge. Well, I still didn't have a computer. I was writing this book on my iPhone. Apparently, I didn't need anything else. But my God knew that I would definitely need motivation to write this book. So He gave me a mentor anyway because I was led back to DeVon Franklin's Instagram page.

The post said: "Do you need a mentor?" (mentor mail)

"Well, yes I do!," I said aloud with conviction. This was some experience I was having. Miraculous! There are no such things as "coincidences," I thought as I smiled. So was it my Father's divine guidance? Dare not only to dream, but to believe! God was showing up in my life big time! Even on my job at the post office. I'd often asked God what was my purpose for being there as I struggled to conform to the daily routine while still juggling the bills. However, I sure was thankful that He was allowing me to work a job while I was working on my dream. You must trust the process as you live each moment. Live in the now because it's the now that will lead you closer to your dream.

When I went to work that week, a lady knocked on the mailroom door to receive an overflow of mail she'd accumulated. I greeted her courteously.

"Hello! How are you?" I asked the lady as I examined her face, because she looked very familiar.

"Fine, thank you," she replied in a somewhat raspy voice.

I smiled as I handed her the mail, while continuing to examine her face. On this day she wore glasses. She was very well-spoken and pleasant. I couldn't stop smiling as I tried to articulate my words as well as she had, changing my normal speech a bit.

"Excuse me mam," I said smiling with amazement, "but has anyone ever told you that you look and sound just like Ms. Maya Angelou?"

"Hah! Hah! Hah!" she laughed slowly. In the meantime I hoped my face wouldn't fall off from smiling as I waited for her to reply.

"Only twice a week," she said in her deep, raspy voice.

Well…you really look like Ms. Maya Angelou," I repeated myself, still in awe.

"Funny thing is, we met in Ghana (West Africa) in 1963, then shared a house with a friend after moving out of the YWCA hostel. We remained friends until she died. That's my friend of fifty-two years," she told me. "Maya mentions me in a book she wrote entitled All God's Children Need Traveling Shoes," Ms. Alice Windom added.

God continued to show His presence, and I was overjoyed and

thankful. I told Ms. Windom about the book I was writing. I thought she might know of someone who could help with editing my book, and didn't want to miss the opportunity to ask her advice. "Well yes I do," she smiled. "I have a friend who will assist you." Ms. Windom wished me well with my book and gave me the name and number of the editor, as well as her own number. In that moment I was thankful and grateful that God placed me at the post office as His plan for my life was leading me closer to my destiny. God allowed me to connect with the great Ms. Windom at the perfect time. God's timing. I call it divine alignment because there is no such thing as a coincidence. I was very grateful not only for Ms. Windom's kindness, but for Ms. Maya Angelou as well.

What does it mean to believe? To accept something as true. It takes courage to believe. Always believe in yourself because God (I Am) will conspire to help you while you're on your journey.

13

Faith

WHAT IS FAITH? "Faith is the substance of things hoped for, the evidence of things not seen" (Hebrews 11:1.). One must have unwavering faith as you search for your true life's purpose or calling. We are God's children who have been sent into the world to serve someone else. It is your service to others that will bring forth fulfillment, happiness, and abundance. Despite life's calamities—regardless of how stressful or tragic—one must not give up on life because it is your faith that will get you through those hard times. You must trust God wholeheartedly and "lean not on your own understanding" because His works far exceed the human mind. And pay attention to the signs; there are always signs of His presence.

Okay, I'll say it again: Faith without works is dead. "Whatever you ask in prayer, you will receive if you have faith" (Matthew 21:22). So stop wandering and wondering and get clear about who you really are because you too are God's child. You see, I am not a victim or a statistic. My story is just one of many stories. But it is because of my story that I'm now connected to millions of people from all walks of life—regardless of race, religion, age, sex, or location. Whether you share my experience of being an orphan or not, we all have feelings, and we have all been met with adversity at some time or another on our life's journey.

It is my intention to not only inspire anyone who has shared my experience of being an orphan, but those of you who have or will be met with misfortune and hardship. I also want to inspire those of you who think that God has forgotten about you. God does not forget about His children. However, you must seek Him, pray, and have faith. Though my life's journey has been turbulent, God was always there with me. It is because of God that you're able to read this book. And it is because of my life challenges that I'm able to share my story without shame, guilt, or embarrassment.

Had I not been shaped and molded by adversity, I would not be able to serve or help anyone else. I had to endure. And although it hurts to lose love ones, I had to endure that as well in order to be able to serve others. Give of yourself and know that your life's experiences do not define who you are. You are valuable. You can do or become whatever you choose. It's up to you to activate the ABR Formula: Ask, Believe, and Receive! Have faith that you have already received. You absolutely must change your thoughts in order to change your life. You are responsible for you!

You see, it was God who reunited my siblings and me, making sure I was in the right places at the right time. It was divine alignment (God's Grace) not "coincidence" that enabled me to meet the individuals I needed to meet to receive the messages I needed to receive. God used me; I prayed for Him to do so. Though I'd been reunited with my siblings, we still struggled financially and were not able to live the life we desired. And yes, it will take time, but I am willing and able to break the chain of poverty and lack!

I am God's child! I am worthy and so are you. I am deserving of the life I want to live, of the life I've envisioned for my family and myself.

I serve a God of abundance, understanding that faith without works is dead. I want to speak to someone out there just as DeVon Franklin spoke out in faith to me: It's somebody out there who put away a dream almost ten years ago! Also, Ms. A's inspired words: Repeat after me with conviction, say: I can, I will, and I am! Their words touched by spirit and fired my determination to never give up.

So never give up on your dreams. Furthermore, it was God who used Buttercup as she gave me book after book saying, "Girl, read the book. You're gonna love it!" When Buttercup lost her book bag, we thought our family dream had died. But God's dream was bigger than our dream as He used me to share not just my story, but a story that has also brought some healing to Buttercup for all she has endured.

In addition, I can now answer Ms. A's question from years ago when I was a young girl. "Baby girl, what is it that you want out of life?" she'd asked me.

Now, as a 37-year-old woman, I can confidently say: "I want to serve. I want to make an impact on someone else's life!" Today I would simply smile and repeat the blessed mantra she'd used to pierce my spirit. I would say to Ms. A with conviction: "I can, I will, and I am!"

In conclusion, I say to you: Don't get discouraged because of circumstances. Create your own circumstances. You are a powerful being—a spirit being having a human experience. You are from the Creator. You are God's child. Therefore, you too have the ability to create. Live the life that you deserve. A life of happiness, fulfillment, and abundance. It was not simply by faith but with work and the ABR Formula that I was able to activate God's help in manifesting this book. It also took self-love and courage to share my story. But most importantly,

I relied on my faith, knowing without a doubt that my dream would come to pass.

So thankful was I for God's love, mercy, favor, and grace that I wanted to express my gratitude for the mighty presence of I Am (God) in my life, and for all that He had done. And so I did the only thing that has **ever** worked in my life. I prayed:

"Dear God, thank you for loving me and seeing me through my adversities. Thank you for watching over my family. Father God, please heal Buttercup. I love her dearly, Lord. Please restore everything that has been taken away from her. And continue to use me, Father. I know now that what I experienced on my journey was for a greater purpose. The purpose for which I was created: To serve!

"Thank you for shaping and molding me, for building my character. Father you made no mistakes, as you had a plan for my life. I cried at times as life unfolded for me without warning, but you were right Father, "for joy cometh in the morning." I know I lacked patience as you shaped and molded me. Thank you Father that I can now give true testimony of my life's path. Thank you for using me, Father. I used to wonder why I was given a life with such difficult trials. But now I'm happy it was me. Why not me? I'm honored to do your work, Lord. The work of serving and helping someone else through their challenges .

"And Father, thank you also for creating me with a sense of humor. I love laughter. It was the laughter that got me through the pain. I'm praying that my story will make it to television, or maybe even to the big screen, Father God. But whatever your will is for my life, let it be done. I want nothing more but for your children to believe and have faith. Father, I know that there will be more for me to do in this earthly realm.

It is not my work but yours. I am only a vessel doing what you have called me to do. Thank you for always being with me, for never leaving me, and for always answering my prayers. Father, I pray that I'm able to reach those that you want me to reach. I pray that I am able to convey and express my story in faith that the message within this book will be received with love as well as bring unity through what we all share: our feelings and emotions.

Father God, I thank you for giving me the strength to endure, for putting me in the position to not only be a blessing to others, but to open doors for myself so that I can better provide for my family. Thank you for conspiring with me to manifest this book. You get all the praise, glory, and gratitude, in Jesus name I pray. Amen."

I continued to sit quietly in solitude after praying—in faith—that the readers would enjoy the book. I am God's child! And as my elders before me have said, "I come as one but I stand for millions!" I smiled with joy as I thought, imagined, and believed that the manifestation of the movie would also come to pass by faith. I began writing out my Father's name in bold print—**G-O-D**.

I heard a subtle voice reply:

"*Go On Dream child, for all things are possible to those who believe in Me.*"

Made in the USA
Monee, IL
16 July 2020